The Story Bible

99 Stories of God's Love

Edward A. Engelbrecht
Gail E. Pawlitz
Editors

CONCORDIA PUBLISHING HOUSE · SAINT LOUIS

Copyright © 2012 Concordia Publishing House
3558 S. Jefferson Ave.
St. Louis, MO 63118-3968
1-800-325-3040 www.cph.org

Edited by Edward A. Engelbrecht and Gail E. Pawlitz

Illustrations by Robert T. Barrett, Robert Papp, Corbert Gauthier, Cheri Bladholm, Greg Copeland, Phil Howe, Robert Hunt, Donald Kueker, and Kevin McCain.

Manufactured in Heshan, China/047365/300309

Library of Congress Cataloging-in-Publication Data
Engelbrecht, Edward.
  The Story Bible : 99 stories of God's love / Edward A. Engelbrecht, Gail E. Pawlitz.
    p. cm.
  ISBN 978-0-7586-1903-7
  1. Bible stories, English. I. Pawlitz, Gail. II. Title.
  BS551.3.E64 2011
  220.5'208—dc22   2010046557

1 2 3 4 5 6 7 8 9 10 11   20 19 18 17 16 15 14 13 12

Contents

THE NEW TESTAMENT

Preface

The Bible remains the most widely read book in history. The benefits of reading it shown at the right are all wonderfully important. Yet above all else, Bible stories lead a child to faith, to prayer, and to life with the heavenly Father and His Son, Jesus Christ, the Savior. We have prepared these Bible stories with special focus on Jesus because He taught,

> You search the Scriptures because you think that in them you have eternal life; and it is they that bear witness about Me. (John 5:39)

Unlike other collections of Bible stories, this book helps children understand THE story of Scripture—the coming of the Savior promised in the Old Testament and the fulfillment of that promise in the New Testament (Jeremiah 31:31–33). Each collection of stories illustrates the Christian faith and life.

Learning to Read with Bible Stories

As we worked for readable wording that young children could understand, we also strove to preserve the unique plot and meaning of each Bible story. Since early readers need to master so many new words, we have studied the text of the Bible with the Dolch and Fry Sight Word lists used by reading teachers. This process helped us simplify the vocabulary for the stories in a consistent way. We have also used another tool for teachers and writers—the Flesch-Kincaid Readability Formula—to help simplify the sentences of the stories. As a result, young children will find these stories simpler to understand than the texts in some other Bible story collections.

Bible stories inspire children's wonder and play.

Bible stories help children learn to read and to apply what they read.

Bible stories lay the foundation for understanding life.

However, these stories are not humdrum accounts that your child will quickly outgrow, nor are they merely paraphrases, which one finds in most other Bible story collections for younger children.

We believe children need texts that are engaging and invite learning. Most young children build vocabulary rapidly. For example, first graders may understand as many as 6,000 spoken words (Paul Kropp, *Raising a Reader* [New York: Doubleday, 1996], 7). Because of these factors and because of our desire to present the biblical text faithfully, we sought to follow the biblical text and preserve rich wording and expressions in the Bible stories. We also introduced each set of Bible stories with visuals and vocabulary that prepare the child for reading the biblical accounts.

Pages 10–12 will help you understand the needs of your child at his or her particular age and ability. These pages also provide strategies that will help you read with your child in a way that is fun and interesting so your child grows with you to understand the Bible as a special, sacred message that your family treasures.

Realistic Illustrations

A trend in Bible story publishing is to illustrate the stories with cartoons, which often present wildly exaggerated characters. Although such illustrations can be fun, they are ultimately misleading to young children.

Appearance matters greatly to children. Researchers have found that children judge whether persons and events in visuals are real by how they appear (Maureen Crago, *Prelude to Literacy* [Southern Illinois University, 1983], 167; Inez Ramsey, "An Investigation of Children's Verbal Responses to Selected Art Styles," *Journal of Education Research* [1989]: 83:47, 51). If a person or event appears unreal in a picture—such as a cartoon—children are likely to conclude that the person or event is unreal. This has important consequences for publications that contain historical persons and events, such as the Bible.

For *The Story Bible*, we sought artists who could provide colorful, child-friendly illustrations that portray biblical characters and events in realistic settings. We believe this is an important message to the children that Jesus is a real person and that the history of His birth, life, death, and resurrection is likewise real. It is our prayer that in every way the message of this collection of stories and illustrations will point to the living Christ who said,

Let the little children come to Me and do not hinder them, for to such belongs the kingdom of heaven. (Matthew 19:14)

Rev. Edward Engelbrecht, S.T.M.
Senior Editor for Professional and Academic Books and Bible Resources

Introduction

The Bible tells many stories.

Some stories are happy.
Some are sad.

Some will surprise you.
A few stories are scary.

But all the stories
are from God.

God's stories show what is good
and what is bad.

But best of all,
they show us . . .

The love of Jesus,

our Savior.

The Bible is all about

Jesus and you.

This Story Bible will

show you how and

why this is true.

The Old Testament

God Creates
the World *part 1*

Genesis 1

In the beginning, God created the heavens and the earth. The earth was without form. It was empty. Darkness was over the face of the deep. And the Spirit of God was hovering over the face of the waters.

God said, "Let there be light." And there was light. God saw that the light was good. God separated the light from the darkness.

God called the light Day. He called the darkness Night. And there was evening and there was morning. It was the first day.

And God said, "Let there be a big space between the waters. Let it separate the waters above from the waters below." And it was so. God called the open space Heaven. And there was evening and there was morning. It was the second day.

creates

empty

hovering

separated

Ask

Who created Day and Night, the Heaven, the Seas, the Earth, and all kinds of plants and trees with seeds?

What did God do to create things?

Do

Roll a ball or toss a beanbag with a partner. As you do so, name something God created that has seeds.

Together say, "I praise You, O God!"

Pray

Dear God, through the power of Your word, You created such a beautiful world. Thank You for it! Amen.

And God said, "Let the waters under the heavens be gathered together into one place. Let the dry land appear." And it was so. God called the dry land Earth. The waters that were gathered together He called Seas. God saw that it was good.

And God said, "Let the earth bring forth plants that make seeds. Let the earth bring forth fruit trees that give fruit in which is their seed. Let each make seeds according to its kind on the earth." And it was so. The earth brought forth plants making seeds according to their own kinds. The earth brought forth trees giving fruit in which is their seed, each according to its kind. And God saw that it was good. And there was evening and there was morning. It was the third day.

God Creates the World *part 2*

Genesis 1–2

God said, "Let there be lights in the heavens to separate the day from the night. Let them be for signs and for seasons. Let them be for days and years. Let them give light upon the earth." And it was so. God made the two great lights and the stars. And God saw that it was good. And there was evening and there was morning. It was the fourth day.

God said, "Let the waters swarm with living creatures. Let birds fly in the heavens." So God created the sea creatures and every living creature in the water. He created every bird. And God saw that it was good. And God blessed them. He said, "Fill the waters in the seas. Let the birds fill the earth." And there was evening and there was morning. It was the fifth day.

swarm

image

God said, "Let the earth bring forth living creatures according to their kinds." And it was so. God made the animals. And God saw that it was good.

Then God said, "Let Us make man in Our image, after Our likeness. Let them rule over the fish and the birds and over the animals."

So God created man in His own image. Male and female He created them.

God blessed them. He said, "Fill the earth. Rule over every living thing." God said, "I have given you every plant and every tree for food." And it was so. God saw everything that He had made. It was very good. And there was evening and there was morning. It was the sixth day.

Thus the heavens and the earth were finished. Everything that filled them was finished. On the seventh day God finished His work and rested. So God blessed the seventh day and made it holy. ❖

Ask

What lights did God make?

What did God put in the water and in the sky?

What did God do when He was finished?

Do

Pretend to be twinkly stars. *Quickly open and close your hands and eyes.*

Pretend to be fish and birds. *Swim with your arms, then flap them as wings.*

Pretend to be land animals. *Hop, jump, crawl, wiggle, or walk.*

Then sit down and rest.

Pray

Dear God,
I believe that You made the heavens and the earth.
I praise You for these good gifts.
Amen.

God Creates Adam and Eve

pleasant

tree of life

tree of the knowledge of good and evil

ashamed

Genesis 2

God formed the man of dust from the ground. He breathed into him the breath of life. Man became a living being.

God planted a garden in Eden. He put the man there. God made every tree pleasant and good for food. The tree of life was in the middle of the garden. So was the tree of the knowledge of good and evil.

A river flowed out of Eden to water the garden.

God put man in the garden of Eden to work it and keep it. God told him, "You may eat of every tree of the garden. But do not eat of the tree of the knowledge of good and evil. If you do, you shall surely die."

Then God said, "It is not good that the man should be alone. I will make a helper for him." God had formed out of the ground every animal and every bird. He brought them to the man to see what he would call them. The man gave names to all the animals and birds.

Ask

What special job did God give to Adam?

How did God make Eve?

Do

God formed Adam from the dust of the ground.

Use play dough to make some creatures.

Can you make your creatures come alive? No. God is the one who gives life.

Pray

Dear God, take care of me and all creation through Your love. Thank You for the love of Jesus, my Savior. Amen.

But there was no helper for Adam. So God caused a deep sleep to come upon the man. While he slept, God took one of his ribs and closed up its place with flesh. God used the rib He had taken from the man to make a woman. Then God brought her to the man. Then the man said,

"At last, this is bone of my bones. This is flesh of my flesh. She shall be called Woman."

Therefore a man shall leave his father and mother. He shall hold on to his wife. They shall become one flesh. And the man and his wife were both naked. But they were not ashamed.

Sin Enters the World

Genesis 3

Now the serpent was tricky. He said to the woman, "Did God really say, 'Do not eat from any tree in the garden'?"

The woman said, "We may eat the fruit of the trees in the garden. But God said, 'Do not eat the fruit of the tree that is in the middle of the garden. Do not even touch it, or you will die.'"

The serpent said, "You will not die. God knows that when you eat the fruit you will be like God. You will know good and evil."

The woman saw that the tree was good for food. She wanted to be wise. So she took its fruit and ate. She gave some to her husband who was with her. And he ate.

Then their eyes were opened. They knew that they were naked. They sewed fig leaves together and made clothes. They hid themselves from God.

But God called to the man. He said, "Where are you? Have you eaten from the tree of which I commanded you not to eat?"

The man said, "The woman gave me fruit from the tree. And I ate."

serpent

evil

cursed

offspring

cherubim

Then God said to the woman, "What have you done?"

The woman said, "The serpent tricked me. And I ate."

God said to the serpent,

"Because you have done this,
    you are cursed.

I will make you and the woman
    enemies.

Her offspring shall bruise your head.
    And you shall bruise His heel."

To the woman God said,

"I will give you pain when you
    have children."

To Adam God said,

"The ground is cursed because of you.

By the sweat of your face you
    shall eat bread.

You will return to the ground.

You are dust. To dust you shall return."

The man called his wife's name *Eve*, because she was the mother of all the living. And the LORD God made clothes for Adam and for his wife. God sent Adam and Eve out of the garden. Near the garden God placed the cherubim and a flaming sword. It turned every way to guard the tree of life. ❧

Ask

Who were the two people who lived in the Garden of Eden?

What wrong thing did they do?

Who took care of them when they left the garden?

What promise did God give to Adam and Eve about her "offspring" (a name for Jesus)?

Do

The devil did not tell Adam and Eve the truth.

Talk about the difference between telling a lie and telling the truth.

Pray

Dear God,
I sin too. I am sorry. Thank You for loving me. Thank You for sending Jesus to take away my sins. Amen.

Noah and the Flood

Genesis 6–7

wickedness

favor

righteous

pitch

covenant

The LORD said, "My Spirit shall not abide in man forever." For the LORD saw that the wickedness of man was great in the earth. He saw that every thought of man's heart was only evil. And the LORD was sorry that He had made man.

So the LORD said, "I will wash away man and animals and creeping things and birds of the heavens from the face of the land. For I am sorry that I have made them."

But Noah found favor in the eyes of the LORD. Noah was a righteous man. He walked with God. And Noah had three sons. Their names were Shem, Ham, and Japheth.

And God said to Noah, "Make yourself an ark of wood. Make rooms in the ark. Cover it inside and out with pitch. Make a roof for the ark. Set the door of the ark in its side. For behold, I will bring a flood of waters upon the earth to destroy all flesh. Everything that is on the earth shall die. But I will have My covenant with you. And you shall come into the ark. So will your sons, your wife, and your sons' wives.

"And you shall bring two of every kind of living thing into the ark. You will keep them alive with you. They shall be male and female. Also store up food."

Noah did all that God commanded him.

Then the LORD said to Noah, "Go into the ark. For in seven days I will send rain on the earth forty days and forty nights."

Noah and his family went into the ark to escape the waters of the flood. And the LORD shut him in.

The flood lasted forty days. And the ark floated on the waters. All the high mountains were covered. And all died: birds, livestock, beasts, all creatures, and all mankind. Only Noah and those who were with him in the ark were left. And the waters stayed on the earth 150 days. ❧

Ask

How did God save Noah and his family?

Who was in the ark with Noah and his family?

How many days and nights did God send rain?

Do

An ark is a big boat like a barge.

Make your own boat. See if it floats.

Pray

Dear God, You loved and protected Noah and his family from all harm and danger. Please love and protect me too. In Jesus' name I pray. Amen.

God's Promise to Noah

Genesis 8–9

God remembered Noah. He remembered all the beasts and all the livestock that were with Noah in the ark. And God made a wind blow over the earth. And the waters began to dry up. At the end of 150 days the waters had gone down. Then the ark came to rest on the mountains of Ararat.

At the end of forty days Noah opened the window of the ark. He sent out a raven. It flew to and fro.

Then Noah sent out a dove to see if the waters were all gone. But the dove found no place to set her foot. And she returned to Noah and the ark.

Noah waited another seven days. And again he sent the dove out of the ark. And the dove came back to him in the evening. And behold, in her mouth was a fresh olive leaf. So Noah knew that the waters had gone down.

raven

to and fro

be fruitful and multiply

covenant

Ask

What did Noah do after he came out of the ark?

What special sign did God put in the sky?

Do

Use watercolor or markers to paint a rainbow.

Pray

Dear God,
You saved Noah and his family. You kept them safe. Thank You for saving me through Jesus, my Savior. Amen.

Then Noah waited another seven days. He sent out the dove once more. And she did not return to him. Noah removed the covering of the ark. He looked. And behold, the ground was dry.

Then God said to Noah, "Go out from the ark. Bring out with you every living thing. Be fruitful and multiply on the earth."

So Noah and his family went out. And all the animals went out by families from the ark. Then Noah built an altar to the LORD. He made offerings on the altar.

And the LORD said in His heart, "I will never again curse the ground because of man. While the earth remains, seedtime and harvest, cold and heat, summer and winter, day and night, shall not stop."

And God blessed Noah and his sons. He said to them, "Be fruitful and multiply and fill the earth."

Then God said to Noah and to his sons, "Behold, I will have My covenant with you. Never again shall there be a flood to destroy the earth." And God said, "This is the sign of the covenant: I have set My rainbow in the cloud."

God Calls Abram

Genesis 12

*God chose people to do special things.
One of those people was Abram.*

Abram lived in the land of Ur. The name
of Abram's wife was Sarai. Now Sarai was
barren. She had no child.

Abram's family wanted to go to the land
of Canaan. But when they came to Haran,
they settled there instead.

One day, the LORD said to
Abram, "Leave your country
and your family. Leave your
father's house. Go to the land
that I will show you. I will
make you into a great nation.
I will bless you and make
your name great. You will be
a blessing. I will bless those
who bless you. I will curse those
who do not honor you. In you all
the families of the earth shall
be blessed."

So Abram went as the LORD
had told him.

Canaan

bless

curse

offspring

pitched

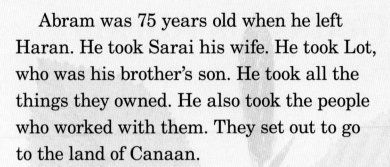

Ask

What did God ask Abram to do?

What did God promise Abram?

Look at the story picture. What is Abram doing at the altar?

Do

Explain the meaning of the word *offspring*.

Make a family tree and talk about your ancestors.

Look at photographs of grandparents and great-grandparents.

Pray

Dear God,
You kept Your promise to care for Abram. Help me remember Your promise to care for me too. Thank You for the blessings You give me through Jesus. Amen.

Abram was 75 years old when he left Haran. He took Sarai his wife. He took Lot, who was his brother's son. He took all the things they owned. He also took the people who worked with them. They set out to go to the land of Canaan.

When they came to the land of Canaan, Abram went to Shechem. At that time the Canaanites lived there. Then the LORD appeared to Abram. He said, "I will give this land to your offspring."

So there Abram built an altar to the LORD. From there Abram moved to the hill country on the east of Bethel. He pitched his tent. He built an altar to the LORD and called upon the name of the LORD. Then Abram went on to where God was leading him.

God's Covenant with Abram

Genesis 15; 17

covenant

vision

shield

heir

After Abram rescued Lot, the word of the LORD came to Abram in a vision. God said, "Fear not, Abram! I am your shield. Your reward shall be very great."

But Abram said, "GOD, what will You give me? I have no child. My heir is a servant in my household."

The word of the LORD came to Abram. God said, "This man shall not be your heir. Your very own son shall be your heir." And God brought Abram outside. God said, "Look toward heaven. Count the stars, if you are able." Then God said to Abram, "This is how many offspring you will have."

Abram believed the LORD.

When Abram was 99 years old the LORD said to him, "Your name shall no longer be called *Abram*. Your name shall be *Abraham*. I have made you the father of many nations. Kings will come from your family."

God said to Abraham, "Call your wife *Sarah*. This shall be her name. I will bless her. I will give you a son by her. She shall become nations. Kings of peoples shall come from her."

Then Abraham fell on his face and laughed. He said to himself, "Shall a child be born to a man who is 100 years old? Shall Sarah, who is 90 years old, bear a child?"

Abram ⟶ Abraham   Sarai ⟶ Sarah

And Abraham said to God, "Oh that my son Ishmael might live before You!"

God said, "No, but Sarah your wife shall give you a son. You shall call his name *Isaac.* I will establish My covenant with him. It will be an everlasting covenant for his offspring after him.

"As for Ishmael, I have heard you. I have blessed him. He shall father twelve princes. I will make him into a great nation. But I will make My covenant with Isaac. He is the son Sarah shall bear to you at this time next year."

The Lord kept His promise of blessings and future kings for the family of Abraham and Sarah. Here are names of some of the kings from their family:

David	Solomon	Hezekiah
Josiah	Jehoiachin	JESUS

The birth of Jesus would fulfill God's promise to bless all nations through Abraham. Jesus is the King of heaven and earth.

Ask

What did God promise to Abram?

What did God tell Abram to look at?

What new names did God give to Abram and Sarai?

Do

On a clear night look for stars and planets in the sky.

Try to count the stars.

Pray

Dear God, You kept Your promises to Abraham. Help me always to believe Your promises. Help me always to trust Your love for me in Jesus, my King. Amen.

Abraham's Visitors from Heaven

**favor
in Your sight**

refresh

knead

Genesis 18

Abraham sat at the door of his tent in the hot part of the day. He looked up. Behold! Three men were standing in front of him.

Abraham ran to meet them. He bowed down. He said, "O Lord, if I have found favor in Your sight, do not pass by. Let me bring a little water and wash your feet. Rest under the tree. I will bring bread. Then you may refresh yourselves. After that you may go on."

They said, "Do as you have said."

Abraham went quickly into the tent to Sarah. He said, "Quick! Knead flour and make cakes."

Abraham ran to the herd and took a calf, tender and good. He gave it to a young man, who prepared it quickly. Then Abraham took the food. He set it before the visitors. He stood by them under the tree while they ate.

The men said to Abraham, "Where is Sarah your wife?"

And he said, "She is in the tent."

Ask

Who talked
to Abraham?

What good news
did God have
for Abraham?

Why did Sarah
laugh?

Is anything
too hard for God?

Do

Abraham and
Sarah had to wait
for a year before
their son would be
born.

How many days
are in a year?

Pray

Dear God,
Abraham and
Sarah waited
a long time for You
to give them
a son. When I have
to wait for You
to answer my
prayers, give me
a faith that trusts
in You. Remind me
that nothing is too
hard for You. In
Jesus' name I pray.
Amen.

The LORD said, "I will come
back to you about this time
next year. Then Sarah your
wife shall have a son."

Sarah was listening at the
tent door behind Him. Now
Abraham and Sarah were old.
So Sarah laughed to herself.

The LORD said to Abraham,
"Why did Sarah laugh? Is
anything too hard for the
LORD? When it is time, I will
return to you. It will be about
this time next year. And Sarah
shall have a son."

The Birth of Isaac

Genesis 18; 21

The LORD said, "Abraham shall surely become a great and mighty nation. All nations of the earth shall be blessed in him. For I have chosen him so he may command his children to keep the way of the LORD. They will do what is right so that the LORD may bring to Abraham what He has promised him."

Abraham prayed. And the Lord listened to Abraham. He heard Abraham's prayers for his nephew Lot. The Lord also delivered Abraham from many troubles.

The LORD visited Sarah as He had said. And the LORD did for Sarah as He had promised. At the time God said, Sarah gave birth to Abraham's son.

Abraham called his son *Isaac*. Abraham was 100 years old when Isaac was born.

Sarah said, "God has made me laugh. Everyone who hears will laugh." And she said, "Who would have said to Abraham that Sarah would nurse children? Yet I have given him a son in his old age."

delivered

cast out

heir

Ask

What did Abraham name his son?

How old was Abraham when his son was born?

What made Sarah laugh?

Do

Count to 100. Did it take a long time?

Abraham had to wait a long time for a son.

Pray

Dear God,
You always do the things You say You are going to do. Help me to trust in You now when I am young and all the days of my life. Amen.

Abraham and Isaac

Genesis 22

tested

provide

thicket

God tested Abraham. He said, "Abraham!"

Abraham said, "Here am I."

God said, "Take your son, your only son Isaac, whom you love. Go to the land of Moriah. Offer him there on one of the mountains."

So Abraham rose early in the morning. He saddled his donkey. He took two of his men with him. He took his son Isaac. He cut the wood for the burnt offering. He went where God told him to go.

On the third day Abraham saw the place. Then Abraham said to his young men, "Stay here with the donkey. We will go there and worship. Then we will come again to you."

Abraham took the wood of the burnt offering. He laid it on Isaac. He took the fire and the knife.

Isaac said to his father, "My father!"

Abraham said, "Here am I, my son."

Isaac said, "We have the fire and the wood. But where is the lamb for a burnt offering?"

42

Ask

Look at the picture. Whom is Abraham hugging?

What is caught in the bush?

Who provided the ram for Abraham's offering?

Do

God is good to me.
Point up to God, then to self.

He provides for all my needs.
Raise up arms.

When I sin,
Hang head.

He forgives me for Jesus' sake.
Raise head and smile.

God is good to me!
Point up to God, then to self.

Pray

Dear God,
You gave Abraham faith to trust You. Help me remember that You will take care of me. Thank You for sending Jesus to pay for my sins. Amen.

Abraham said, "God will provide the lamb, my son." So they went on together.

When they came to the place of which God had told him, Abraham built the altar. He laid the wood in order. He bound Isaac his son. Abraham laid Isaac on the altar on top of the wood.

Then Abraham took the knife. But the angel of the LORD called to him from heaven. He said, "Abraham, Abraham!"

Abraham said, "Here am I."

He said, "Do not lay your hand on the boy. For now I know that you fear God. You have not kept your son, your only son, from Me."

Abraham looked up. Behind him was a ram. It was caught in a thicket by his horns.

Abraham took the ram. He offered it as a burnt offering. So Abraham called that place "The LORD will provide."

And the angel of the LORD said to Abraham, "I will bless you. I will multiply your offspring. They will be as many as the stars and as the sand on the seashore. Through you all people will be blessed."

Isaac and Rebekah

Genesis 24

When Abraham was old, he said to his servant, "Go to my country and to my kindred. Find a wife for Isaac."

The servant took ten of his master's camels and left. He also took gifts from his master. He went to the city of Nahor. There he made the camels kneel by the well at evening. It was the time when the women draw water.

And he said, "O LORD, let a young woman come to whom I say, 'Please give me a drink.' Then she shall say, 'Drink, and I will water your camels.' Let her be the one You have chosen for Isaac."

Before he had finished, Rebekah came. She was very attractive. She went down to the spring and filled her jar. Then the servant said, "Please give me a little water."

She said, "Drink, my lord." And she gave him a drink. Then she said, "I will water your camels." So she got water for all his camels. The man gazed at her in silence.

kindred

gazed

kinsmen

veil

When the camels finished, Abraham's servant gave her gifts. He said, "Whose daughter are you? Is there room in your father's house to spend the night?"

She said, "I am the daughter of Bethuel. We have plenty of room."

The man said, "The LORD has led me to my master's kinsmen."

Rebekah had a brother named Laban. He said, "Come in. I have prepared the house and a place for the camels."

So the man came. He told Laban all that had happened. Then Laban said, "The thing has come from the LORD. Take Rebekah and go. Let her be the wife of your master's son."

Abraham's servant brought out gifts.

In the morning, Rebekah and her women rode camels and followed the man.

Now Isaac was living in the Negeb. He went out in the field toward evening. And he saw camels coming. Rebekah saw Isaac. She said, "Who is that man walking to meet us?"

The servant said, "It is my master." So she took her veil and covered herself.

The servant told Isaac all that he had done. Then Rebekah became Isaac's wife. And Isaac loved her.

Ask

What job did Abraham give his servant?

Look at the picture. What is the woman's name?

Why did she take such a long trip?

Whom will this woman marry?

Do

Look through family pictures. Talk about the family God gave you.

Pray

Thank You, dear God, for making Isaac and Rebekah a family. Thank You for giving me a family too. Thank You for making me part of Your Church family. Amen.

Jacob and Esau

Genesis 25; 27

birthright

game

garments

trembled

Isaac and Rebekah had twins. Esau grew up to be a hunter. Jacob was a quiet man. Isaac loved Esau. But Rebekah loved Jacob.

Once when Jacob was cooking, Esau said, "Let me eat some stew. For I am exhausted!"

Jacob said, "Sell me your birthright now."

So Esau sold his birthright to Jacob. Then Jacob gave Esau bread and stew.

When Isaac was old and could not see, he called Esau. He said, "Go and hunt game. Prepare food. Bring it to me, so I may bless you before I die."

Rebekah was listening. She said to Jacob, "Bring me two goats. I will prepare them so your father may bless you."

But Jacob said, "Esau is a hairy man. I am smooth."

His mother said, "Obey me and go."

So Rebekah prepared food. Then she took the garments of Esau and put them on Jacob. She put the skins of the goats on his hands and his neck. She put the food into Jacob's hand.

Ask

Look at the story picture. What did Jacob bring Isaac?

What does Jacob have on his arms?

What is Isaac doing?

What will happen when Esau brings food to his father?

Do

Use a blindfold to cover your eyes.

Touch and feel the difference between the arms of two people.

Pray

Dear God,
You forgave Jacob. Thank You for always forgiving me too. Thank You for all the blessings that You give to me, especially for Jesus.
Amen.

So he went to his father. Jacob said, "I am Esau. Eat so you may bless me."

But Isaac said, "Come near."

So Jacob went near. Isaac said, "The voice is Jacob's. But the hands are the hands of Esau. Are you really Esau?"

Jacob answered, "I am."

Then Isaac said, "Bring the food, that I may eat."

Then Isaac said, "Come and kiss me." So Jacob came and kissed him. Isaac smelled his garments. And he blessed him. As soon as Isaac blessed Jacob, he left.

Then Esau came. He brought food too. And he said, "Father, eat, that you may bless me."

Isaac said, "Who are you?"

Esau answered, "I am Esau."

Isaac trembled. He said, "Who came? I have blessed him?"

Esau cried out, "Bless me, Father!"

But Isaac said, "Your brother tricked me. He has taken your blessing."

Esau said, "He has cheated me two times. He took away my birthright. Now he has taken away my blessing."

Jacob's Dream

Genesis 27–28

Now Esau hated Jacob because his father had blessed Jacob. Esau said, "After the days of mourning for my father, I will kill Jacob."

Rebekah heard this news. She said to Jacob, "Your brother is planning to kill you. Flee to my brother. Stay with him until your brother's anger goes away."

Then Isaac called Jacob. He blessed him. Isaac said, "You must not take a wife from the Canaanite women. Go to the house of your mother's father. Take your wife from there. God bless you." So Isaac sent Jacob away.

Jacob came to a certain place and stayed there that night. The sun had set. Taking one of the stones, he put it under his head.

mourning

flee

offspring

vow

Ask

What did Jacob dream?

What special news did God give Jacob?

What did Jacob do when he woke up?

Do

Sit on the bottom step of a stairway.

Each time you think of a new place where God is with you, scoot up one step.

Do this until you get to the top step.

Pray

Dear Father, You loved Jacob. You watched over him. Thank You for loving me too. Thank You for promising to be with me wherever I go. Amen.

Jacob lay down to sleep. And he dreamed. He saw a ladder set up on the earth. The top of it reached to heaven. The angels of God were ascending and descending on it! And the LORD stood above it.

He said, "I am the LORD, the God of Abraham and the God of Isaac. The land on which you lie I will give to you and to your offspring. In you and your offspring shall all the families of the earth be blessed. I am with you. I will keep you wherever you go. I will bring you back to this land. For I will not leave you."

Then Jacob awoke from his sleep. He said, "Surely the LORD is in this place. And I did not know it." And he said, "How awesome is this place! This is the house of God. This is the gate of heaven."

In the morning Jacob took the stone and set it up. He poured oil on it. He named that place *Bethel*.

Then Jacob made a vow. He said, "If God will be with me and will keep me, so that I come again to my father's house in peace, then the LORD shall be my God. This stone, which I have set up for a pillar, shall be God's house. And of all that You give me I will give a full tenth to You."

Joseph and His Brothers

Genesis 37

Jacob lived in the land of Canaan. God changed his name to "Israel." He had twelve sons who would become the twelve tribes of Israel. This is the story of his sons.

Joseph was 17 years old. He was caring for the flock with his brothers. He brought a bad report about his brothers to their father.

Israel loved Joseph more than any of his sons. He made Joseph a robe of many colors. But when his brothers saw that their father loved him more, they hated Joseph.

Now Joseph had a dream. When he told it to his brothers, they hated him even more. He said to them, "Hear this dream: We were binding sheaves in the field. My sheaf arose and stood upright. Your sheaves bowed down to mine."

His brothers said, "Are you to rule over us?" So they hated Joseph even more.

Then Joseph dreamed another dream. He told his brothers, "The sun, the moon, and eleven stars were bowing down to me." And his brothers were jealous of Joseph.

Israel

binding

sheaves

caravan

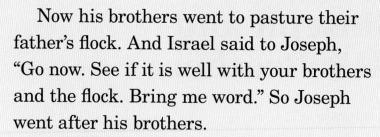

Ask

Tell about the story picture.

What did Joseph's brothers do to him?

Do

Put on your best robe. Tell one of Joseph's dreams.

Pray

Dear Jesus, I am sorry for the times that I get angry and act mean. Thank You for forgiving me and taking care of me all the time. Amen.

Now his brothers went to pasture their father's flock. And Israel said to Joseph, "Go now. See if it is well with your brothers and the flock. Bring me word." So Joseph went after his brothers.

His brothers saw Joseph from afar. They said, "Here comes this dreamer. Let us kill him."

But Reuben said, "Throw him into this pit." So when Joseph came, they took off his robe of many colors. And his brothers threw him into a pit. And looking up they saw a caravan with camels on the way to Egypt.

Then Judah said, "Let us sell our brother to the caravan." His brothers listened. And they sold Joseph for silver.

Then the brothers killed a goat. They dipped the robe in the blood. They brought the robe to their father. They said, "Tell us if this is your son's robe."

And their father said, "It is my son's robe. An animal has eaten Joseph. He is torn to pieces." Then Jacob tore his robe. He wept for his son.

Joseph was sold in Egypt to Potiphar.

Joseph's Troubles

Genesis 39

Now Joseph had been brought to Egypt. And Potiphar, the captain of the army, bought him.

The LORD was with Joseph. He became a successful man in the house of his master. Joseph was in charge of all that Potiphar had in house and field. The master had no worry about anything but the food he ate.

Now Joseph was handsome. And after a time his master's wife said, "Lie with me."

But Joseph said no to his master's wife. He said, "How can I do this very bad thing? How can I sin against God?"

Day after day, Joseph would not listen to her. But one day, he went into the house to work. No other men were there. She caught his robe. She said, "Lie with me." But Joseph left his robe in her hand. He ran out of the house.

His master's wife saw that Joseph had left his robe. She called to the men of her house.

Potiphar

successful

master

fled

kindled

Ask

Did Potiphar believe his wife's lie about Joseph?

What did Potiphar do to Joseph?

Who was with Joseph when he had troubles?

Do

Hug someone. Say, "When troubles come, and we are sad, God loves and cares for us."

Pray

Dear God, when Joseph had troubles, You took care of him. When I have troubles, help me remember that You love me and will care for me too. In Jesus' name I pray. Amen.

She said, "See, Joseph came to me. I cried out with a loud voice. As soon as he heard me, he left his robe. Joseph fled. He left the house."

Then she kept Joseph's robe until Potiphar came home. She told him the same story. She said, "The Hebrew servant came to laugh at me. But as soon as I called out, he left his garment beside me. He fled from the house."

As soon as Potiphar heard his wife, his anger was kindled. And Joseph's master put him into the prison. It was the place where the king's prisoners were kept.

But the LORD was with Joseph. The LORD showed him steadfast love. The keeper of the prison put Joseph in charge of all the prisoners. Whatever was done there, Joseph was the one who did it. And whatever Joseph did, the LORD made it succeed.

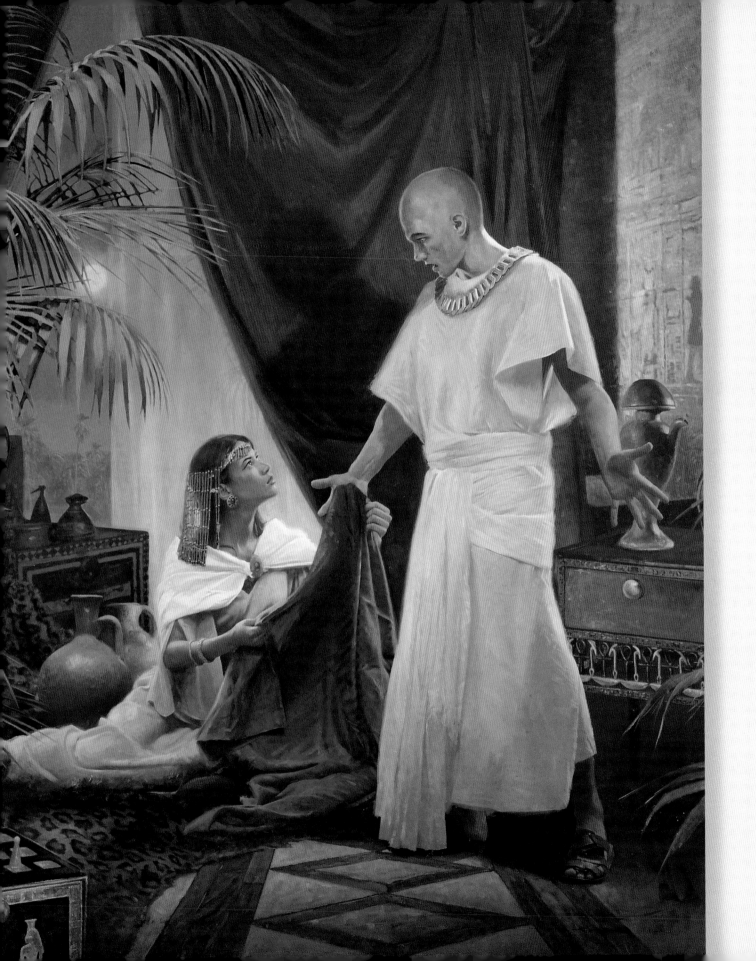

Joseph Feeds Egypt

Genesis 40–41

The king's cupbearer and baker were in prison with Joseph. One night they both dreamed. In the morning they said, "No one can tell us the meaning of our dreams."

Joseph said, "Tell the dreams to me."

The cupbearer said, "In my dream there was a vine. On the vine were three branches. Its blossoms ripened into grapes. I pressed the grapes into the king's cup. I put the cup in his hand."

Then Joseph said, "It means in three days Pharaoh will make you his cupbearer. Remember me when it is so."

Then the baker said, "I also had a dream. There were three baskets on my head. In the top basket were baked foods for Pharaoh. But the birds ate out of the basket."

Joseph said, "The three baskets are three days. In three days Pharaoh will hang you."

It happened just as Joseph said. But the cupbearer forgot about Joseph.

After two years, Pharaoh dreamed that he was standing by the Nile River. Out of the Nile River came seven plump cows.

 cupbearer

Pharaoh

plump

famine

Ask

What did the king see in his dream?

Who helped Joseph tell the king about his dream?

What did Joseph do to help many people?

Do

God used Joseph to make sure there was food for many people.

God can use you, too, to provide food for others. What could you do?

Pray

Dear Father, You helped Joseph take care of many people. Thank You for sending people to take care of me too. Thank You for all the food You give me. Thank You especially for Jesus, my Savior. Amen.

Seven thin cows came after them. The thin cows ate up the plump cows.

Then Pharaoh dreamed a second time. Seven plump ears of grain were growing on one stalk. After them grew seven thin ears. The thin ears ate up the plump, full ears.

In the morning, Pharaoh called for the magicians and wise men. None could tell him the meaning of the dreams. Then the cupbearer told Pharaoh about Joseph.

Pharaoh sent for Joseph. He said to Joseph, "No one can tell me the meaning of my dream. I have heard you can."

Joseph said, "It is not me. God will answer."

Pharaoh told Joseph both dreams. Joseph said, "There will come seven years of plenty in Egypt. But after them will come seven years of famine. Select a wise man to gather food in these good years. That food shall be extra for years of famine."

This plan pleased Pharaoh. He said to Joseph, "Since God has shown you all this, you shall do this good work."

During the good years, Joseph saved up grain. Then the years of famine began. Joseph opened the storehouses. People from many places came to buy grain.

Joseph Forgives

Genesis 42–45

When Jacob learned that there was grain in Egypt, he said to his sons, "Buy grain for us there."

Joseph was the one who sold grain to all the people of the land. And Joseph recognized his brothers. But they did not recognize him. Joseph gave them food. But he tested them. Joseph made them leave Simeon behind. And they had to bring Benjamin, the youngest brother, to Joseph.

The brothers were sad to leave Simeon. They said, "We are guilty for what we did to Joseph." They returned home.

The famine was very bad. Sometime later, Jacob said, "Go again. Buy food." So the brothers and Benjamin went to Egypt. They stood before Joseph.

Joseph had a meal for his brothers. He brought Simeon. At the meal Joseph asked, "Is your father still alive?"

They said, "He is still alive."

Joseph also saw Benjamin. Then Joseph left the room. He wept.

After the meal, Joseph told a servant, "Fill the men's sacks with food.

grain

famine

overtake

63

Ask

What did Jacob tell his sons to buy in Egypt?

Were the brothers happy, sad, or afraid when they found out the ruler was Joseph?

What did Joseph tell his brothers so they would not be afraid?

Do

Make a forgiveness flag. On a triangle-shaped piece of paper, draw a cross on one side. On the other side draw a heart.

Remember God helps us forgive people in our family who hurt us.

Pray

Dear God, thank You for forgiving me. Help me to show love and forgive others. For Jesus' sake I pray. Amen.

"Put each man's money in his sack. Put my silver cup in the sack of the youngest." And the servant did as he was told.

The brothers left. Now Joseph said to his servant, "Follow after the men. When you overtake them, say, 'Why have you repaid evil for good? You have done evil.' "

The servant overtook the brothers. He told them what Joseph said. The brothers said they had not taken the cup. But the cup was found in Benjamin's sack. So the brothers returned to the city. They feared that Benjamin would become a servant.

Judah went to Joseph. He said, "Please do not be angry with me. If we come home without Benjamin, our father will die. Make me your servant instead."

Then Joseph wept. He said, "I am Joseph! Is my father still alive?"

His brothers could not answer. They were afraid. So Joseph said, "I am your brother, Joseph, whom you sold. Do not be worried or angry because you sold me. God sent me before you to save lives.

"Go to my father. Say, 'God has made Joseph lord of all Egypt. Come to me. I will provide for you.' " And Joseph kissed all his brothers and wept.

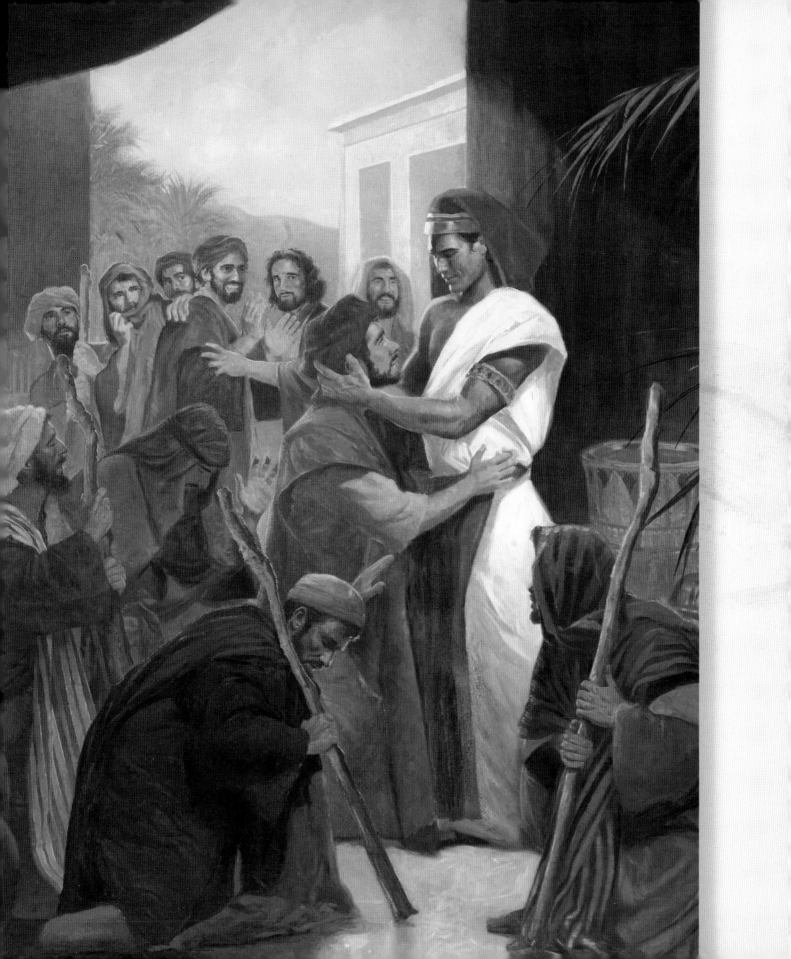

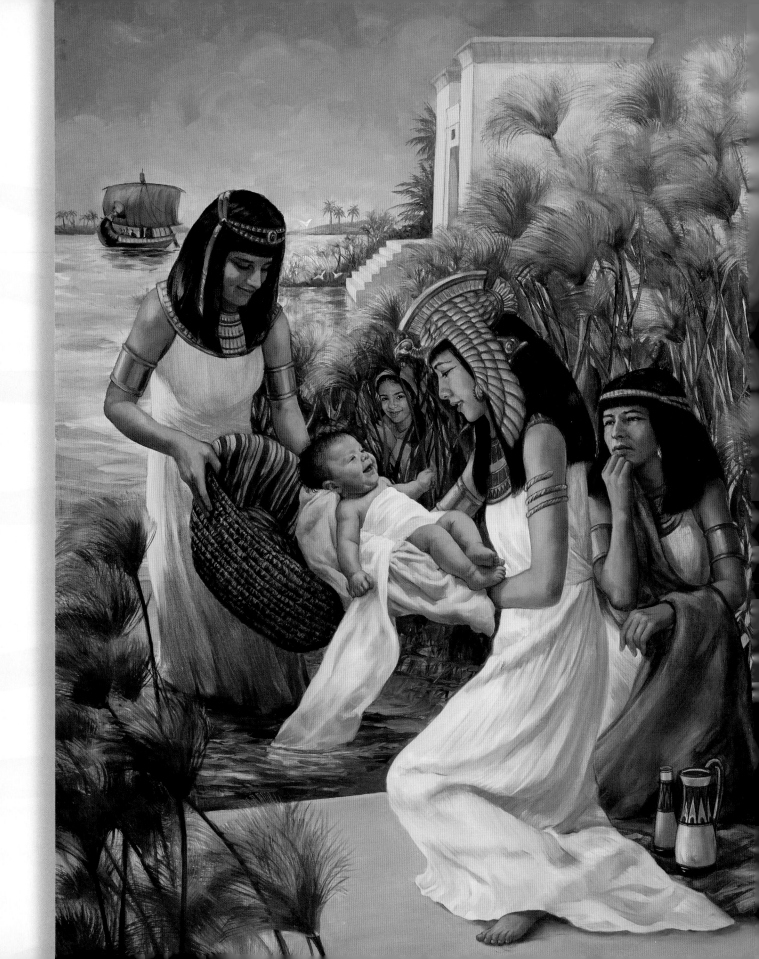

The Birth of Moses

Exodus 1–2

The sons of Israel who came to Egypt had many children. They grew strong. They lived in many places in the land.

Now there was a new king over Egypt. He did not know Joseph.

And the new king said, "The people of Israel are too many. They are too mighty for us. Let us make a wise plan to deal with them."

They put slave masters over the people of Israel. The masters gave them heavy burdens. So they made the people of Israel work as slaves.

Then Pharaoh told his people, "Every son that is born to the Hebrews you shall throw into the Nile River."

Now a Levite woman gave birth to a son. She hid him three months. When she could hide him no longer, she made a basket of bulrushes. She covered it with tar. She put the child in it. She put the basket among the reeds by the riverbank.

The baby's sister stood at a distance. She wanted to know what would happen to him.

masters

bulrushes

reeds

bathe

Ask

Look at the story picture. Who is in the basket?

Who is holding the baby?

Who is in the grasses, peeking?

Do

Moses' sister helped to take care of him.

How can you help take care of a baby?

Pray

Dear God, thank You for saving Moses. Thank You for sending Jesus to save me from my sins. Amen.

Now the daughter of Pharaoh came down to bathe at the river. Her young women walked beside the river. Pharaoh's daughter saw the basket among the reeds. She sent her servant to take it.

When she opened it, she saw the child. The baby was crying. Pharaoh's daughter took pity on him. She said, "This is one of the Hebrews' children."

Then the child's sister said, "Shall I call a Hebrew woman to nurse the child for you?"

And Pharaoh's daughter said, "Go."

So the girl went to the child's mother.

And Pharaoh's daughter said to the mother, "Take this child away. Nurse him for me. I will give you wages."

So the woman took the child. And when the child grew up, she brought him to Pharaoh's daughter. Then he became her son. She named him *Moses*. ❦

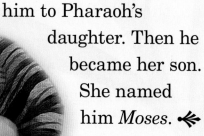

Moses and the Burning Bush

Exodus 2–4

When Moses had grown up, he had to leave Egypt. He lived in the land of Midian. There he was a shepherd. Back in Egypt, the people of Israel had to work hard as slaves. So they asked God for help.

Moses was keeping the flock of his father-in-law. He led his flock to Horeb, the mountain of God. And the LORD appeared in a flame of fire out of a bush. Moses looked. He saw the bush was burning. But the bush was not burning up.

God called, "Moses, Moses!"

And Moses said, "Here I am."

Then God said, "Do not come near. Take your sandals off. This is holy ground."

And He said, "I am God."

Moses was afraid to look at God.

Then the LORD said, "I have seen My people in Egypt. I know their sufferings. I will send you to bring My people out of Egypt."

serpent

cloak

But Moses said, "Who am I that I should go to Pharaoh? Who am I that I should bring the children of Israel out of Egypt?"

God said, "But I will be with you."

Then Moses answered, "But they will not believe me."

The Lord said, "What is in your hand?"

Moses said, "A staff."

God said, "Throw it on the ground." So Moses threw it. It became a serpent. Then Moses put out his hand. It became a staff.

Again, the Lord said, "Put your hand inside your cloak." When Moses did, his hand was white like snow. Then God said, "Put your hand back inside your cloak." When Moses took it out, it was like the rest of his flesh.

But Moses said, "Oh, my Lord, I am slow of speech."

Then the Lord said, "Aaron, your brother, can speak well. I will teach you both what to do. He shall speak for you. And take your staff. You shall do the signs with it."

Moses went back to his father-in-law Jethro. He said to him, "Please let me go back to my brothers in Egypt."

Jethro said to Moses, "Go in peace."

Ask

What does Moses see in the bush?

What does God tell Moses to do?

What does God promise Moses?

How does God talk to us?

Do

Watch a lit candle. Notice how the wick burns and the wax drips.

When God talked to Moses in the burning bush, it did not burn up. God has power over everything.

Pray

Dear God,
You spoke to Moses in a burning bush. You speak to me in Your Word, the Bible. Help me to listen and to do what the Bible says. In Jesus' name I pray. Amen.

Moses and the Plagues

plagues

redeem

staff

gnats

Exodus 5–10

Moses and Aaron said to Pharaoh, "Thus says the LORD, 'Let My people go.' "

But Pharaoh said, "Who is the LORD that I should obey Him? I will not let Israel go. Why do you take the people away from their work?"

The same day Pharaoh said, "You shall no longer give the people straw to make bricks. Let them gather the straw."

Then Moses said, "O Lord, why have You done this? For Pharaoh has done evil."

But the LORD said, "Now you shall see what I will do to Pharaoh. Say to the people, 'I will redeem you. I am the LORD, who has brought you out of slavery.' "

Moses spoke this to the people of Israel. But they did not listen.

So the LORD said to Moses, "Tell Pharaoh to let the people of Israel go. Pharaoh will not listen to you. Then I will bring My people out of Egypt by great acts. The Egyptians shall know that I am the LORD."

Ask

Who has to work hard for Pharaoh?

What did Moses tell Pharaoh?

What great acts did God do so that Pharaoh would let the people go?

Do

God wanted the Egyptians to know that He was the true God.

Tell someone what the true God has done for you.

Pray

Dear God,
You took good care of Your people. You take good care of me. I am so happy You sent Jesus to be my Savior.
Thank You.
Amen.

Then the LORD said, "When Pharaoh says, 'Do a miracle,' say to Aaron, 'Take your staff. Throw it down. It will become a serpent.'"

So Moses and Aaron did just as the LORD said. And the staff became a serpent. But Pharaoh would not listen.

Then the Lord did many great acts so the Egyptians would know that He was God. First, He made the waters to be blood. But Pharaoh did not let the people go.

Then God sent frogs. But Pharaoh did not let the people go. Next God sent gnats. After that He sent flies. Then the horses, donkeys, camels, herds, and flocks died.

Still, Pharaoh would not let the people go. So God let the people and animals get sores called boils. God sent hail. Then locusts ate up the plants. Finally, there was darkness for three days. But Pharaoh still would not let the people go.

Then Pharaoh said to Moses, "Get away. Take care never to see my face again. For on that day you shall die."

Moses said, "As you say! I will not see your face again." ←

The Passover

Exodus 11–13

The LORD said to Moses, "I will bring one more plague upon Pharaoh and upon Egypt. Then he will let you go. Speak now to the people."

So Moses said, "Thus says the LORD: About midnight I will go out in the midst of Egypt. And every firstborn in the land of Egypt shall die. There shall be a great cry throughout all the land of Egypt. Then you may know that the LORD makes a difference between Egypt and Israel."

The LORD said to Moses and Aaron, "This month shall be the first month of the year for you. Kill some lambs at twilight. Then take some of the blood and put it on the doorposts of the houses. Eat the meat that night, roasted on the fire. You shall eat the lamb with your belt on, your sandals on your feet, and your staff in your hand. And you shall eat it in a hurry. It is the LORD's Passover.

Passover

plague

twilight

strike

pillar

75

"For I will pass through the land of Egypt that night. I will strike all the firstborn in the land of Egypt. I am the LORD. The blood shall be a sign for you on the houses where you are. And when I see the blood, I will pass over you."

Then Moses called all the elders of Israel. He said to them, "Go and kill the Passover lamb."

At midnight the LORD struck down all the firstborn in the land of Egypt. The LORD struck down the firstborn of Pharaoh. And there was a great cry in Egypt. For there was not a house where someone was not dead.

Then Pharaoh told Moses and Aaron, "Up! Go out from among my people. Go, serve the LORD, as you have said. Be gone. And bless me also!"

God led the people toward the Red Sea. And they camped at the edge of the wilderness. The LORD went before them by day in a pillar of cloud. And by night there was a pillar of fire to give them light.

Ask

What did God tell Moses the people should put around the door?

Where did the people go?

Do

At dinner tonight, wear your sandals.

Talk about the special meal the people of Israel ate.

Pray

Dear God, thank You for saving Your people. Thank You for sending Jesus to save me from my sins. Amen.

Crossing the Red Sea

chariot

salvation

Exodus 14–15

Then the LORD said to Moses, "Tell Israel to camp by the sea. I will harden Pharaoh's heart. He will chase them. And I will get glory over Pharaoh and all his army. Then the Egyptians shall know that I am the LORD."

And the king of Egypt said, "What is this we have done? We have let Israel go from serving us." So he made ready his chariot. And Pharaoh took his army with him.

And behold, the Egyptians were marching. And the people of Israel feared greatly. And they cried out to the LORD.

But Moses said to the people, "Fear not. Stand firm. See the salvation of the LORD. The LORD will fight for you."

The LORD said to Moses, "Tell the people of Israel to go forward. Lift up your staff, and stretch out your hand over the sea and divide it. Then the people of Israel may go through the sea on dry ground."

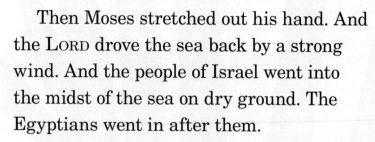

Ask

How did the people of Israel get across the water?

Who chased them?

Who saved the people of Israel?

Do

Can you part water? Try to part the water when you wash the dishes or take a bath.

Talk about how God saved His people.

Pray

Dear God,
You were with Your people. You saved them from their enemies. Thank You for sending Jesus to save me from my sins.
Amen.

Then Moses stretched out his hand. And the LORD drove the sea back by a strong wind. And the people of Israel went into the midst of the sea on dry ground. The Egyptians went in after them.

Early in the morning the LORD looked down on the Egyptian forces. He scared the Egyptians.

And the Egyptians said, "Let us flee from before Israel. For the LORD fights for them."

Then the LORD said to Moses, "Stretch out your hand over the sea. Then the water may come back upon the Egyptians."

So Moses stretched out his hand. And the sea returned.

Thus the LORD saved Israel that day from the Egyptians. So the people feared the LORD. And they believed in the LORD and in His servant Moses.

Then Moses and the people of Israel sang this song:

"The LORD is my strength and my song.
  And He has become my salvation.
This is my God. I will praise Him.
This is my father's God. I will exalt Him.
The LORD is a man of war.
The LORD will reign forever and ever."

God Provides Quail and Manna

Exodus 16

The people of Israel came to the wilderness of Sin. And the people of Israel grumbled. They spoke against Moses and Aaron, "Would that we had died in the land of Egypt! But you have brought us out into this wilderness to kill us with hunger."

Then the LORD said to Moses, "Behold, I am about to rain bread from heaven for you. The people shall go out and gather a portion every day. I will test them. I want to see if they will walk in My law or not."

quail

manna

wilderness

grumbled

dew

So Moses and Aaron said to the people, "At evening you shall know that it was the LORD who brought you out of Egypt."

In the evening quail came and covered the camp. The people caught the quail to eat them.

81

And in the morning dew lay around the camp. And when the dew had dried up, there was a fine, flake-like thing. It was like frost on the ground. The people said to one another, "What is it?"

And Moses said to them, "It is bread. The LORD has given this to you to eat. The LORD has commanded: 'Gather of it, each one of you, as much as he can eat.'"

And the people of Israel did so. They gathered, some more, some less.

And Moses said to them, "Let no one leave any of the bread over till the morning." But they did not listen to Moses. Some left part of it till the morning. And it had worms in it. The bread stank. And Moses was angry with them.

Now the people of Israel called its name *manna*. It was like seed. It was white. The taste of it was like wafers made with honey. The people of Israel ate the manna forty years. They ate it till they came to the land of Canaan.

Ask

What problem did the people have?
What did God give them to help?

Do

Manna was a kind of bread that had a taste of honey.
Taste some bread with honey on it.

Pray

Dear God,
You gave food and water to Your people. You give me everything I need, too, including Jesus as my Savior. Amen.

The Ten Commandments

Exodus 19–20

covenant

consecrate

jealous

The people of Israel came into the wilderness of Sinai. There Israel camped before the mountain. Then Moses went up to God.

The LORD said, "Tell the people of Israel: You yourselves have seen what I did to the Egyptians. Now therefore, obey My voice and keep My covenant. Then you shall be My treasured people. And you shall be to Me a kingdom of priests and a holy nation.

"Behold, I am coming to you in a thick cloud. Then the people may hear when I speak with you. They may also believe you forever.

"Go to the people. Consecrate them today and tomorrow. Let them wash their clothes. Let them be ready for the third day."

On the morning of the third day there was thunder and lightning. A thick cloud was on the mountain. There was a loud trumpet blast. All the people in the camp trembled.

Moses spoke. God answered him in thunder. The LORD called Moses to the top of the mountain. And Moses went up.

Ask

What happened when God came to the mountain?

Where did Moses go to talk with God?

What rules did God give the people of Israel?

Do

Say the Ten Commandments.

Pray

Dear God,
You loved Your people. You wanted them to love and respect You and others. Help me to do that too. Amen.

And God spoke all these words, saying,

"I am the LORD your God, who brought you out of the land of Egypt, out of the house of slavery.

"You shall have no other gods before Me. You shall not make for yourself a carved image. You shall not bow down to them or serve them. For I the LORD your God am a jealous God.

"You shall not take the name of the LORD your God in vain.

"Remember the Sabbath day, to keep it holy.

"Honor your father and your mother.

"You shall not murder.

"You shall not commit adultery.

"You shall not steal.

"You shall not bear false witness against your neighbor.

"You shall not covet your neighbor's house.

"You shall not covet your neighbor's wife, or his male servant, or his female servant, or his ox, or his donkey, or anything that is your neighbor's."

The Ways of God

Exodus 33–34; 40

The people of Israel soon broke God's Law. They made the Lord angry with their sin.

The LORD said to Moses, "Go up to the land I promised to Abraham, Isaac, and Jacob. Go up to a land flowing with milk and honey. But I will not go with you. For you are a stiff-necked people."

When the people heard this, they were sad.

But Moses said to the LORD, "Please show me Your ways. Consider too that this nation is Your people."

And the LORD said to Moses, "I will make all My goodness pass before you. I will proclaim before you My name 'The LORD.' But you cannot see My face. For man shall not see Me and live. While My glory passes by I will cover you with My hand. Then I will take away My hand. You shall see My back. But My face shall not be seen."

So Moses rose early in the morning. He went up on Mount Sinai.

stiff-necked people

merciful

gracious

abounding

tabernacle

The LORD passed before Moses. And He said, "The LORD, the LORD, a God merciful and gracious. He is slow to anger. He is abounding in steadfast love and faithfulness. He keeps steadfast love for thousands, forgiving sin. But He will by no means clear the guilty."

So Moses quickly bowed his head toward the earth. He worshiped God. And Moses said, "O Lord, please forgive our sin. Let us be Your people."

And the LORD said to Moses, "Write these words. I have made a covenant with you and with Israel."

Later, the LORD spoke to Moses. He said, "You shall build the tabernacle. And you shall put in it the ark of the covenant, a table, a lampstand and lamps, and a golden altar for incense. Place a basin between the tent and the altar. Put water in the basin."

The tabernacle would be the house of worship for Israel. The glory of the Lord would fill it. God would lead the people of Israel. He would go with them to the Promised Land.

Ask

What did God say about the ways He works with people?

What special place did God tell Moses to build?

What beautiful things were in the tabernacle?

How did God show that He was with the people?

Do

Moses and God talked so Moses could learn more about God.

Find out more about someone you love. Ask this person two questions.

Pray

Dear God, You showed Moses Your ways. You showed him that You love Your people and forgive their sin. O Lord, I know You love me too. Please forgive my sin. Amen.

The Twelve Spies in Canaan

spy

cluster

Numbers 13–14

The LORD spoke to Moses. He said, "Send men to spy out the land of Canaan. I am giving the land to Israel. From each tribe you shall send a man."

So Moses sent twelve men. From the tribe of Judah, he sent Caleb. From the tribe of Ephraim, he sent Joshua.

Moses said, "Go see the land. See if the people who live in it are strong or weak. Be of good courage. And bring some of the fruit of the land."

So they went. They spied out the land. They cut down a branch with a single cluster of grapes. And they carried it on a pole between two of them! They also brought some other kinds of fruit.

At the end of forty days they returned from spying out the land. They showed all the people of Israel the fruit. And they told Moses, "The land flows with milk and honey. This is its fruit. However, the people who dwell in the land are strong. The cities are forts and very large."

Ask

What did the spies bring back from the Promised Land?

What did they see that made them afraid?

Which men trusted God to be with them and help them?

Do

Talk about times when you were afraid.

Talk about times when you were brave.

Remember God loves us all the time, no matter how we feel.

Pray

Dear God, sometimes I get scared. I am so happy that You still love me. Make me brave like Caleb and Joshua. Thank You for sending Jesus to save me from my sins. Amen.

But Caleb quieted the people. He said, "Let us go up at once! For we are well able to win."

Then other spies said, "We are not able. For they are stronger than we are." So they brought to the people of Israel a bad report of the land. They said, "The land eats up people who live there. All the people that we saw in it are very tall. We seemed small like grasshoppers."

Then all the people wept that night.

But the glory of the LORD appeared. And the LORD said to Moses, "How long will this people not believe in Me?"

Moses said, "Please pardon the sin of this people, according to Your steadfast love."

Then the LORD said, "I have pardoned, according to your word. But they have put Me to the test ten times. Not one shall come into the land except Caleb and Joshua."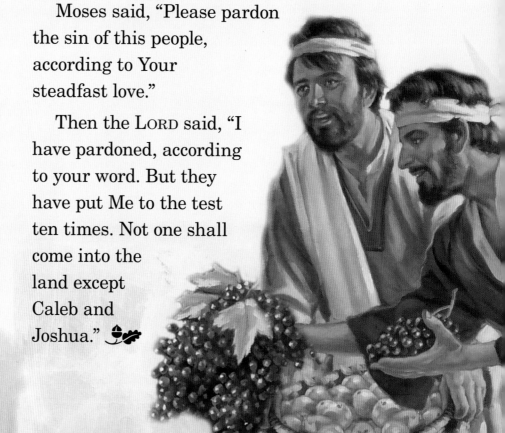

The Bronze Serpent

Numbers 21; 33

The people of Israel lived in the wilderness for 40 years. When they sinned, God punished them. Moses taught them to repent and trust in the Lord. He taught them to worship the Lord. But sometimes the people still grumbled.

repent

impatient

plains

Once, the people of Israel set out by the way to the Red Sea. They would go around the land of Edom. But the people became impatient on the way. And the people spoke against God and against Moses. They said, "Why have you brought us up out of Egypt to die in the wilderness? For there is no water. And we hate this worthless food."

Then the LORD sent fiery serpents among the people. The serpents bit the people. Many people of Israel died.

So, the people came to Moses. They said, "We have sinned. For we have spoken against the LORD and against you. Pray to the LORD. Ask Him to take away the serpents from us." So Moses prayed for the people.

And the LORD said to Moses, "Make a fiery serpent. Set it on a pole. And everyone who is bitten, when he sees it, shall live."

So Moses made a bronze serpent. He set it on a pole. And if a serpent bit anyone, he would look at the bronze serpent. Then he would live.

When the people came to the plains of Moab, the LORD spoke to Moses. He said, "Speak to the people of Israel. Say, 'When you pass over the Jordan River, you shall settle in the land. For I have given the land to you.'

"But if you do not drive out the people of the land, they will be thorns in your sides. They shall trouble you."

God told Moses these and other commands about how to live in the Promised Land.

Ask

What does God tell Moses to do to help the people who were bitten by the serpents?

What will happen to the people who look at the serpent on the pole?

Who saves us from our sins?

Do

Make serpent rattles. Fill a small container with dried beans. Secure the lid.

Now read the story again. Shake the container when you hear the word *serpent*.

Pray

Dear God, help me to say "I'm sorry" when I grumble and fuss. Thank You for loving me and forgiving me for Jesus' sake. Amen.

Good-bye, Moses

Deuteronomy 18; 34

Levi

minister

prophet

swore

wisdom

Moses taught Israel about the Promised Land in a sermon.

"The priests and all the tribe of Levi shall have no land in Israel. They shall eat the LORD's food offerings that you shall give them. For they will stand and minister in the name of the LORD.

"You shall not learn to act like the other nations. For the LORD your God is driving them out before you.

"The LORD your God will raise up for you a prophet like me. He will be from among you. He will be from your brothers. You shall listen to Him. The LORD said to me, 'I will put My words in His mouth. He shall speak to them all that I command Him.'"

Then Moses went up from the plains of Moab. He climbed Mount Nebo, which is not far from Jericho. And the LORD showed him all the land. Moses saw as far as the western sea. He saw the hills and the Plain, that is, the Valley of Jericho.

Ask

What did Moses tell the people about a prophet?

Where did God take Moses?

What did Moses see?

Then what happened to Moses?

Do

God promised to speak to His people through prophets. God speaks to you through His Word.

Pick out a favorite Bible story in this book.

What is God telling you in that story?

Pray

Dear God,
You let Moses see the Promised Land before he died. Give me faith to believe in Your promises. Give me faith to believe in the gift of heaven that You have given to me through Jesus. Amen.

And the LORD said, "This is the land I swore to Abraham, to Isaac, and to Jacob that I would give. I said, 'I will give it to your family.' I have let you see it with your eyes. But you shall not go over there."

So Moses the servant of the LORD died. He died, according to the word of the LORD. The LORD buried him in the valley in the land of Moab. But no one knows the place of his burial to this day. Moses was 120 years old when he died. His eyes were still good. He was still strong.

Israel wept thirty days for Moses.

And Joshua was full of the spirit of wisdom. For Moses had laid his hands on him. So the people of Israel followed Joshua. And there has not been a prophet in Israel like Moses. The LORD knew Moses face to face. None did all the signs and the wonders that the LORD sent Moses to do in the land of Egypt.

Rahab Believes

Joshua 2

Joshua sent two men as spies. He said, "Go, view the land, especially Jericho."

In Jericho, they came into the house of Rahab. And the king of Jericho was told, "Behold, men of Israel have come here tonight to search out the land."

Then the king sent a message to Rahab. He said, "Bring out the men who have come to you. They have come to search out all the land."

But the woman took the men up to the roof. She would hide them with the stalks of flax that she had laid on the roof.

Before the men lay down to hide, she said, "I know that the LORD has given you the land. The fear of you has fallen upon us. For we have heard how the LORD dried up the Red Sea before you when you came out of Egypt. And as soon as we heard it, our hearts melted. For the LORD your God, He is God in the heavens and on the earth.

"Please swear to me by the LORD. Say that you will be kind to my father's household. Give me a sign that you will save my family and deliver our lives from death."

spies

stalks of flax

swear

deliver

scarlet

And the men said to her, "Our life for yours even to death! If you do not tell on us, then when the LORD gives us the land, we will be kind to you."

Then she let them down by a rope through the window. And she said to them, "Go into the hills. Hide there three days. Then you may go your way."

The men said, "Behold, when we come into the land, you shall tie this scarlet cord in the window. You shall gather your family into your house."

And she said, "So be it." Then she sent them away. And she tied the scarlet cord in the window.

The two men returned to Joshua. They said, "Truly the LORD has given all the land into our hands."

Ask

Where did the spies go?

What did Rahab do for the spies?

What did Rahab believe about God?

What did the spies promise to do for Rahab?

Do

Rahab tied a scarlet cord in the window so she could be saved.

How did God save you?

Use a red ribbon to make a cross.

Pray

Dear God, Rahab believed that You were God. Rahab believed that You saved her. Thank You for giving me faith to believe in You. Thank You for saving me from my enemies. Amen.

Entering the Promised Land

ark of the
covenant

priests

exalt

heap

Joshua 3–4

The people of Israel set out. They came to the Jordan.

At the end of three days the officers went through the camp. They told the people, "You will see the ark of the covenant of the LORD your God. The priests will carry it. Then you shall set out from your place. Follow the ark."

Joshua said to the people, "Wash yourselves. For tomorrow the LORD will do wonders among you."

The LORD said to Joshua, "Today I will begin to exalt you in the sight of all Israel. Then they may know that, as I was with Moses, so I will be with you."

And Joshua said to the people, "Come here. Listen to the words of the LORD your God.

Ask

Where were the people of God going?

How does God help them cross the river?

God promises to take us to a new home too. What is it called?

Do

Twelve men picked up twelve stones. Joshua piled them up to remember what God had done.

Ask each person in your family to bring one rock, block, or can of food to make a stack.

Talk about what God has done for you.

Pray

Dear Jesus, help me always to remember what You have done for me. Thank You for taking away my sins so that I can go to heaven someday. Amen.

"Here is how you shall know that the living God is among you. Behold, the ark of the covenant of the Lord of all the earth. The ark is passing over before you into the Jordan. The feet of the priests carrying the ark shall rest in the waters of the Jordan. Then the waters shall be cut off from flowing. The waters coming down from the river shall stand in one heap."

So the people set out. Soon the feet of the priests bearing the ark were dipped in the water. Then the waters coming down the river stopped. And the people passed over by Jericho.

The LORD said to Joshua, "Take twelve men from the people. Take a man from each tribe. Command them. Say, 'Take twelve stones out of the midst of the Jordan.' "

And Joshua set up the twelve stones. He placed them where the feet of the priests bearing the ark of the covenant had stood.

And the LORD said to Joshua, "Command the priests bearing the ark to come up out of the Jordan."

The priests came up. Then the waters returned to their place, as before.

The Fall of Jericho

Joshua 6

Jericho was shut up. None went out. None came in.

And the LORD said to Joshua, "See, I have given Jericho into your hand. You shall march around the city. All the men of war shall go around the city once. You shall do this for six days. Seven priests shall bear seven trumpets of rams' horns before the ark. On the seventh day you shall march around the city seven times. The priests shall blow the trumpets. They will make a long blast with the ram's horn. Then all the people shall shout with a great shout. Then the wall of the city will fall down flat."

So Joshua said to the people, "Go forward. March around the city. Let the armed men pass on before the ark of the LORD."

priests

trumpets of rams' horns

ark of the LORD

relatives

fame

But Joshua commanded the people, "You shall not shout. Neither shall any word go out of your mouth until the day I tell you to shout. Then you shall shout."

So Joshua caused the ark of the LORD to circle the city, going about it once. So they did for six days.

On the seventh day the people rose early. They marched around the city in the same way seven times. Then Joshua said to the people, "Shout! For the LORD has given you the city. Only Rahab and all who are with her in her house shall live. For she hid the messengers whom we sent."

To the two men who had spied out the land, Joshua said, "Go into Rahab's house. Bring her out and all who belong to her. Do as you swore to her." And they brought Rahab and all her relatives. They put them outside the camp of Israel. And they burned the city with fire.

And Rahab has lived in Israel to this day. For she hid the messengers whom Joshua sent to spy out Jericho. So the LORD was with Joshua. His fame was in all the land.

Ask

What did God tell the people to do?

Who made the walls fall down?

How does God help you?

Do

God told the priests to blow trumpets. Play your favorite instrument.

Pray

Dear God, You helped the people of Israel. You are my helper too. You have saved me from all my enemies of sin, death, and the devil by sending Jesus to die on the cross. I am so thankful. Amen.

Gideon

Judges 6

wheat

valor

forsaken

strike

Baal

The people served the LORD all the days of Joshua. Then there arose other generations. They did not know the LORD. So the LORD raised up judges. They saved Israel. This is the story of a judge.

The angel of the LORD came and sat under a tree. Gideon was hiding wheat from the Midianites. And the angel of the LORD said to Gideon, "The LORD is with you, O mighty man of valor."

And Gideon said to him, "Please, sir, if the LORD is with us, why has Midian attacked us? Our fathers said, 'Did not the LORD bring us up from Egypt?' But now the LORD has forsaken us."

And the LORD said, "Go in this might of yours. Save Israel from the hand of Midian."

And Gideon said, "Please, LORD, how can I? Behold, I am the least in my father's house."

And the LORD said to him, "But I will be with you. You shall strike the Midianites."

That night the LORD said to Gideon, "Take your father's bulls and pull down your father's altar of Baal. Build an altar to the LORD your God."

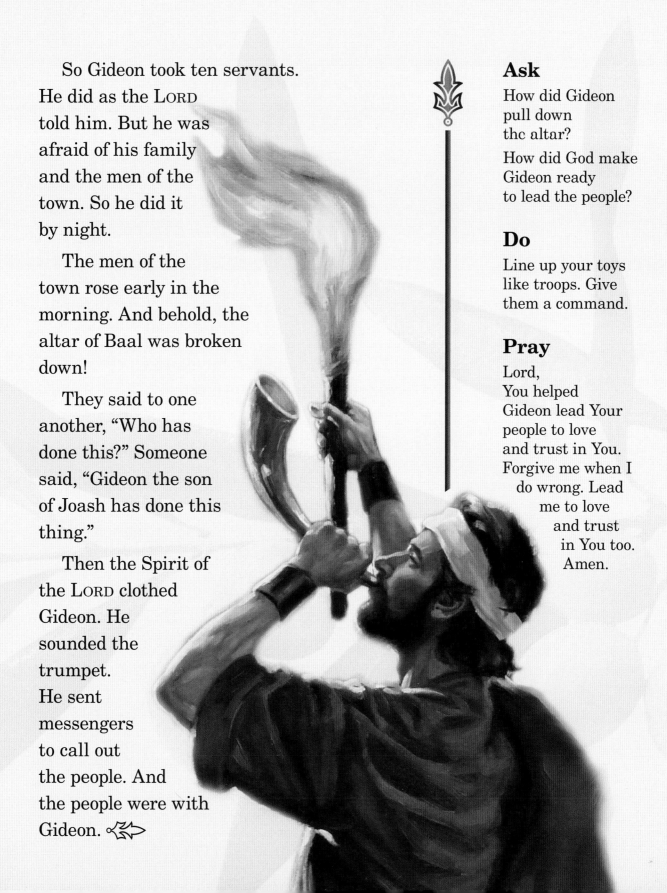

So Gideon took ten servants. He did as the LORD told him. But he was afraid of his family and the men of the town. So he did it by night.

The men of the town rose early in the morning. And behold, the altar of Baal was broken down!

They said to one another, "Who has done this?" Someone said, "Gideon the son of Joash has done this thing."

Then the Spirit of the LORD clothed Gideon. He sounded the trumpet. He sent messengers to call out the people. And the people were with Gideon.

Ask

How did Gideon pull down the altar?

How did God make Gideon ready to lead the people?

Do

Line up your toys like troops. Give them a command.

Pray

Lord, You helped Gideon lead Your people to love and trust in You. Forgive me when I do wrong. Lead me to love and trust in You too. Amen.

A Sword for the LORD

boast

companies

pursued

subdued

Judges 7–8

The LORD said to Gideon, "The people with you are too many. Do not let Israel boast, saying, 'My own hand has saved me.' Now proclaim to the people, 'Whoever is afraid, return home.'" Only 10,000 remained.

The LORD said to Gideon, "The people are still too many. Take them down to the water. I will test them."

So Gideon brought the people down to the water. And the LORD said to Gideon, "Some will lap the water with the tongue, as a dog laps. Set him by himself. Likewise, set aside everyone who kneels down to drink."

And the number of those who lapped, putting their hands to their mouths, was 300. But all the rest knelt down to drink.

The LORD said to Gideon, "With the 300 men I will save you. Let the others go home."

Gideon divided the 300 men into three companies. He put trumpets into the hands of all of them and empty jars. There were torches inside the jars.

Ask

How many soldiers did God tell Gideon to use?

Whom does Gideon trust to win the battle?

Do

Make a torch. Roll craft paper into a tube. Overlap and tape the edges. Push a piece of yellow tissue paper in the top.

Hold up the torch. Say, "For the Lord!"

Pray

Dear Jesus, You helped Gideon win the battle. Help me each day when I have troubles. Thank You for dying on the cross and rising from the dead to win the victory for me over sin, death, and the devil. Amen.

And Gideon said to them, "Look at me, and do likewise. When I come to the outside of the camp, do as I do. I will blow the trumpet, I and all who are with me. Then you blow the trumpets also. Blow them on every side of all the camp. Shout, 'For the Lord and for Gideon.'"

So Gideon came to the camp. They blew the trumpets. They smashed the jars. And they cried out, "A sword for the Lord and for Gideon!"

Every man of Israel stood in his place around the camp. But all the army of Midian ran. They cried out and fled. Then Gideon's men pursued Midian.

So Midian was subdued before the people of Israel. And the land had rest forty years in the days of Gideon.

Ruth Goes Home with Naomi

Ruth 1–2

When the judges ruled, there was a famine in the land. A man of Bethlehem went to live in Moab. He went with his wife Naomi and his two sons. But the man died. Later, both sons died.

Then Naomi heard that the LORD had visited His people. He had given them food. Naomi said to her two daughters-in-law, "Go, and each of you return to her mother's house. May the LORD deal kindly with you."

But they said to her, "No, we will return with you to your people."

But Naomi said, "Turn back, my daughters. Why will you go with me?" Then they lifted up their voices and wept. And Orpah kissed her mother-in-law good-bye.

But Ruth clung to Naomi. Ruth said, "Do not tell me to leave you. For where you go I will go. Where you lodge I will lodge. Your people shall be my people, and your God my God."

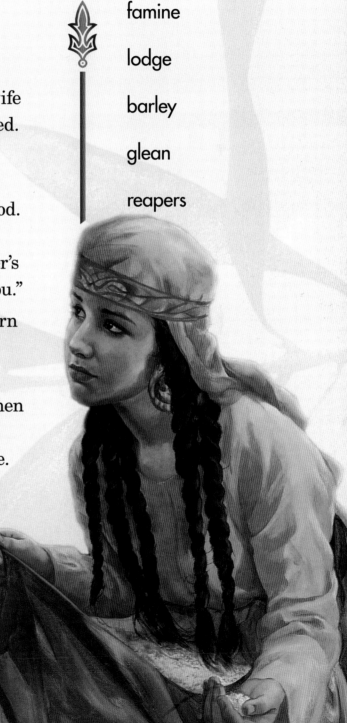

famine

lodge

barley

glean

reapers

So the two of them went to Bethlehem at the beginning of barley harvest. Ruth said to Naomi, "Let me go to the field and glean among the ears of grain."

And Naomi said to her, "Go, my daughter."

And Ruth happened to come to the field belonging to Boaz.

Boaz came from Bethlehem. He said to the workers, "The LORD be with you!"

They answered, "The LORD bless you."

Then Boaz said to his young man who was in charge of the reapers, "Whose young woman is this?"

And the servant said, "She is the young Moabite woman. She came back with Naomi. She has worked hard from early morning until now, except for a short rest."

Boaz said to Ruth, "All that you have done for your mother-in-law since the death of your husband has been fully told to me. The LORD repay you for what you have done."

Then Ruth said, "I have found favor in your eyes, my lord. You have comforted me. You have spoken kindly to your servant." So Ruth gleaned in the field until evening. ⤙⤚

Ask

What work did Ruth do so she and Naomi could eat?

Who is the man who helped Ruth and Naomi?

Do

Boaz let Ruth pick grain from his field so she could eat.

You can share food with people too.

Pray

Dear God, thank You for giving me my family to love and care for me. Thank You for loving me so much that You sent Jesus to be my Savior. Amen.

A Blessing for Ruth

Ruth 2–4

threshing

redeemer

parcel

witnesses

renowned

Naomi said to Ruth, "Where did you glean today? Blessed be the man who took notice of you." Ruth told her mother-in-law she had worked with Boaz.

And Naomi said to Ruth, "May he be blessed by the LORD."

So Ruth kept close to the women of Boaz.

Naomi said to Ruth, "My daughter, should I seek rest for you? Then it may be well with you. Is not Boaz our relative? See, he is working tonight at the threshing floor."

So Ruth went down to the threshing floor. Ruth told Boaz, "I am Ruth, your servant. And you are a redeemer for Naomi's land."

He said, "May you be blessed by the LORD, my daughter. I will do all that you ask. Yet there is a redeemer nearer than I. If he is not willing to redeem you, then, I will redeem you."

The next day, Boaz went up to the gate. He sat down there. And behold, the redeemer, of whom Boaz had spoken, came by.

Boaz said to the redeemer, "Naomi has come back from Moab. She is selling a parcel of land. If you will not redeem it, tell me. There is no one besides you to redeem it, and I come after you."

The redeemer said, "Take my right of redemption. For I cannot redeem it."

Then Boaz said to the elders, "You are witnesses this day. I have bought the land from the hand of Naomi. Also Ruth the Moabite I have bought to be my wife."

So Boaz took Ruth. She became his wife. And the LORD gave her a son. Then the women said to Naomi, "Blessed be the LORD! He has given you this day a redeemer. May his name be renowned in Israel!"

Then Naomi took the child. She laid him on her lap. She became his nurse. They named him Obed. He was the father of Jesse, the father of David.

Ask

How did Boaz help Naomi and Ruth?

What blessing did God give to Ruth?

Do

Boaz bought some land and then got permission to marry Ruth.

Pretend you are getting married. What will you promise to do?

Pray

Dear Lord,
You blessed Ruth with a home and a family. Bless my family in the love of Jesus, the Son of David.
Amen.

Hannah's Prayer

1 Samuel 1–2

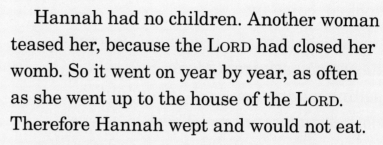

womb

vowed

weaned

anointed

Hannah had no children. Another woman teased her, because the Lord had closed her womb. So it went on year by year, as often as she went up to the house of the Lord. Therefore Hannah wept and would not eat.

Elkanah, her husband, said to her, "Hannah, why do you weep? And why do you not eat? And why is your heart sad? Am I not more to you than ten sons?"

Hannah was deeply sad. She prayed to the Lord. She vowed a vow and said, "O Lord, will You remember me and not forget Your servant? Please give me a son. Then I will give him to the Lord all the days of his life."

As she continued praying before the Lord, Eli saw her mouth. Hannah was speaking in her heart. But her lips moved, and her voice was not heard. Therefore Eli took her to be a drunken woman.

But Hannah answered, "No. I am not drunk. But I have been pouring out my soul before the Lord."

Then Eli answered, "Go in peace. God grant your prayer."

Ask

What did Hannah ask God to give her?

When she was at the tabernacle, who told Hannah to "Go in peace"?

What did God give to Hannah?

Do

Hannah prayed at the tabernacle, a kind of church.

You can thank and praise God too. When you sit down at church, you can say a prayer too.

Pray

Dear God, You heard Hannah's prayer. You gave her a child at just the right time. Thank You for hearing all my prayers. Thank You for giving me what is good for me at just the right time. Amen.

Then Hannah went her way and ate. Her face was no longer sad.

And the LORD remembered her. And in time Hannah bore a son. She called his name *Samuel*.

When she had weaned him, Hannah took Samuel to the house of the LORD at Shiloh. They brought the child to Eli. Hannah said, "For this child I prayed. The LORD has answered my prayer to Him. Therefore I am giving him to the LORD. As long as he lives, he belongs to the LORD."

Samuel worshiped the LORD there. And Hannah prayed and said,

"The LORD raises up the poor
     from the dust.

He lifts the needy from the ash heap
     to make them sit with princes
     and have a seat of honor.

The LORD will judge
     the ends
     of the earth.

He will give
     strength
     to His king
     and exalt the
     power of His
     anointed."

120

God's Promise

1 Samuel 2

Now the sons of Eli were bad men. They did not know the LORD. The sin of the young men was great in the sight of the LORD. The men mistreated the offering of the LORD.

Samuel was serving the LORD while a boy. And his mother used to make for him a little robe. She would take it to him each year when she went up with her husband. And the young man Samuel grew in the presence of the LORD.

Now Eli was very old. He kept hearing all that his sons were doing to all Israel. And he said to them, "Why do you do such things? For I hear of your evil works from all the people."

But his sons would not listen to the voice of their father.

Now the young man Samuel continued to grow. He grew in size and in favor with the LORD and also with man.

presence

scorn

anointed

Ask

What bad thing did Eli's sons do?

What gift did Samuel get from his mother?

What promise did the man of God make?

Do

Put on your robe. Join your family in a prayer.

Pray

Dear Lord, let me grow up to love You and Your Word. Help me to worship faithfully in Your name forever. Amen.

Then there came a man of God to Eli. He said to him, "Why do you scorn My sacrifices and My offerings? Why do you honor your sons above Me? I will raise up for Myself a faithful priest. He shall do according to what is in My heart and in My mind. And I will build him a sure house. He shall go in and out before My anointed forever."

God Calls Samuel

1 Samuel 3

Eli's eyesight had begun to grow dim, so he could not see. Eli was lying down in his place. And Samuel was lying down in the temple of the LORD, where the ark of God was.

Then the LORD called Samuel. He said, "Here I am!"

And Samuel ran to Eli. He said, "Here I am. For you called me."

But Eli said, "I did not call. Lie down again." So Samuel went and lay down.

And the LORD called again, "Samuel!"

Samuel arose. He went to Eli. He said, "Here I am. For you called me."

But Eli said, "I did not call, my son. Lie down again."

Now Samuel did not yet know the LORD. The word of the LORD had not yet been revealed to him.

And the LORD called Samuel the third time. And he arose and went to Eli. He said, "Here I am. For you called me."

revealed

blaspheming

vision

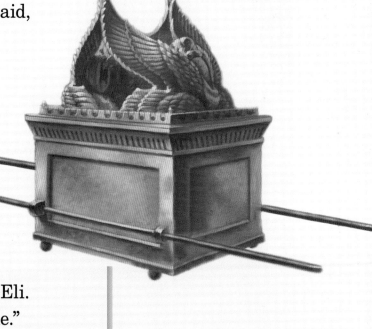

123

Then Eli knew that the LORD was calling the young man. Therefore Eli said to Samuel, "Go, lie down. If He calls you, you shall say, 'Speak, LORD. For Your servant hears.' " So Samuel went and lay down in his place.

And the LORD came and stood. He called as at other times, "Samuel! Samuel!"

And Samuel said, "Speak. For Your servant hears."

Then the LORD said to Samuel, "Behold, I am about to punish Eli's house forever." His sons were blaspheming God. And Eli did not stop them."

And Samuel was afraid to tell the vision to Eli.

But Eli said, "Do not hide it from me."

So Samuel told him everything.

And Eli said, "It is the LORD. Let Him do what seems good to Him."

And Samuel grew. And the LORD was with him.

Ask

Where did Samuel serve God?

Who talked to Samuel in the night?

What does God tell us through the Bible?

Do

Learn bedtime prayers so that you can talk to God at night too.

Pray

Dear Jesus, thank You for my pastor who teaches me about Your love. Help me to serve You too. Amen.

Samuel Anoints David

anoints

chosen

ruddy

1 Samuel 16

The LORD said to Samuel, "Fill your horn with oil, and go. I will send you to Jesse in Bethlehem. Anoint for Me the one whom I show you."

Samuel did what the LORD commanded him. He came to Bethlehem. Samuel looked on Jesse's oldest son. He thought, "Yes! The LORD's anointed is standing before Him."

But the LORD said to Samuel, "Do not look on him or on his height. I have rejected him. For the LORD sees not as man sees. The LORD looks on the heart."

Then Jesse called another son. He made him walk by. Samuel said, "The LORD has not chosen this one." Then Jesse made another son pass by. And Samuel said, "The LORD has not chosen this one." Jesse made seven of his sons pass before Samuel.

126

Samuel said to Jesse, "The LORD has not chosen these."

Then Samuel said to Jesse, "Are all your sons here?"

And Jesse said, "There is the youngest. Behold, he is keeping the sheep."

Samuel said to Jesse, "Send and get him. We will not sit down till he comes here." And Jesse sent for David.

David was ruddy. He had beautiful eyes. He was handsome.

The LORD said to Samuel, "Arise, anoint him." Then Samuel took the horn of oil. He anointed David while his brothers watched. From that day forward, the Spirit of the LORD was upon David.

Ask

What job did God give Samuel?

What job did God give David?

What is the surprise in the story?

Do

When David was very young, God chose David to do an important job.

What jobs can you do?

Make a list. Ask God to help you do those things.

Pray

Dear Jesus, thank You for choosing me to be Your special child. Amen.

David Sees the Army

1 Samuel 17

Philistines

champion

war cry

The Philistines wanted a war. They had a champion named Goliath. He was nine feet tall! He had a helmet on his head. He wore a coat of metal. He had armor on his legs. He held a big spear.

Goliath shouted to Israel, "Why have you come out to battle, you servants of Saul? Choose a man. Let him come down to me. If he is able to kill me, then we will be your servants. But if I kill him, then you shall be our servants." When Saul and all Israel heard this, they were afraid.

The three oldest sons of Jesse went to the battle. So Jesse said to David, "Take some food. Go see if your brothers are well."

David came to the camp. The army was going out, shouting the war cry. David ran to his brothers. As he talked with them, Goliath the champion came. He spoke the same words as before. And David heard him.

All the men of Israel were afraid. But David said, "Who is this Philistine, that he should talk like that about God?"

David's oldest brother heard what David asked. He was angry with David. He said, "Why have you come and left the sheep? You have come to see the battle."

And David said, "What have I done wrong?"

Ask

How tall was Goliath?

What did Goliath shout to the army of Israel?

Do

Goliath was very tall.

How tall are you? Have someone measure how tall you are.

Pray

Dear Jesus, when people are mean to me or say bad things about You, please help me to say what is right and true. Amen.

David Fights Goliath

struck

slung

1 Samuel 17

David said, "I will go and fight with this Philistine."

Saul said to David, "You are not able to fight with him. He is a man of war."

But David said, "I used to keep sheep for my father. Sometimes a lion or a bear came and took a lamb. I went after him. I struck him and saved the lamb out of his mouth. I struck down both lions and bears. This Philistine shall be like one of them. The LORD saved me from the paw of the lion. The LORD saved me from the paw of the bear. He will save me from this Philistine."

Saul said to David, "Go, and the LORD be with you!" Then Saul put a helmet, a coat of metal, and a sword on David.

David tried them. Then David said, "I cannot go with these." So David took them off. David took his staff. He chose five smooth stones from the brook. He put them in his pouch. David's sling was in his hand. He went to the Philistine.

Ask

What did Saul want David to wear when David went out to fight Goliath?

What did David use to kill Goliath?

What did David learn to do as a shepherd that helped him win?

Do

Draw a slingshot and some stones.

These are little things. God can use little things to do big jobs. He can use little people too.

Pray

Dear Jesus, thank You for helping little people with big problems. Amen.

When the Philistine saw David, he made fun of him. The Philistine said, "Am I a dog, that you come to me with your staff? I will give your flesh to the birds and the beasts."

Then David said to the Philistine, "You come to me with a sword and with a spear. But I come to you in the name of the LORD, the God of Israel. This day the LORD will stop you. I will strike you down. Then all the earth may know that there is a God in Israel. The battle is the LORD's. He will give you into our hand."

David ran. He put his hand in his bag. He took out a stone. He slung the stone and struck the Philistine on his forehead. The Philistine fell on his face.

When the Philistines saw that their champion was dead, they fled. The men of Israel rose with a shout. They chased the Philistines away.

Saul said to David, "Whose son are you, young man?"

David said, "I am the son of your servant Jesse of Bethlehem."

David and Jonathan Become Friends

1 Samuel 18

After David killed the giant Goliath, King Saul was pleased. He had David come and live with him. David fought against more enemies. In this story, listen to find out the special ways that God took care of David.

As soon as David had finished speaking to King Saul, the soul of Jonathan was tied to the soul of David. Jonathan loved him as his own soul.

Saul took David home that day. He would not let David return to his father's house. Then Jonathan made a covenant with David. Jonathan took off his robe. He gave it to David. Jonathan also gave David his armor and even his sword. He gave David his bow and belt.

soul

covenant

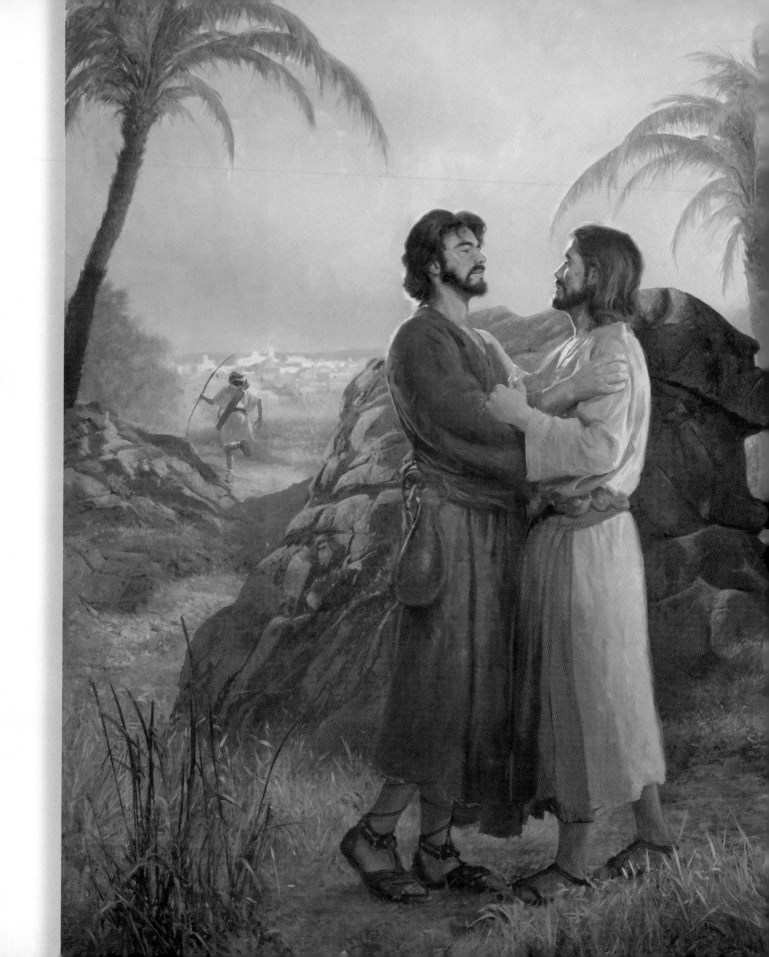

David went out and did well wherever Saul sent him. So Saul put David over the other men of war. This was good in the sight of all the people. It was also good in the sight of Saul's servants.

Sometime later, God used David's good friend Jonathan to help save David from great danger. God gave these two men a special friendship.

Ask

Tell about the friends in the story.

Who are your friends?

Do

Friends love each other. They do kind things. Jesus showed His love and kindness for you by dying on the cross for your sins.

List the names of your friends.

Thank God for each one.

Pray

Dear Jesus, thank You for my friends. Help me to love them. Amen.

Solomon Builds the Temple

1 Kings 5–6

 cedars

cypress

foundation

cherubim

Solomon sent word to King Hiram, "David my father could not build a house for the name of the LORD his God. War surrounded him. Yet the LORD put the enemies under the soles of his feet.

"Now the LORD my God has given me rest on every side. So I will build a house for the name of the LORD my God. Now therefore command that cedars of Lebanon be cut for me. My servants will join your servants in the work."

Hiram rejoiced greatly. He said, "Blessed be the LORD this day. He has given to David a wise son to be over this great people. My servants shall bring trees to you." So Hiram sold Solomon all the timber of cedar and cypress that he desired.

At King Solomon's command, workers also cut great, costly stones. They would lay the foundation of the house of the LORD. So 480 years after Israel came out of Egypt, Solomon began to build the house of the LORD.

Ask

What did the
people use to build
the temple?

What parts of the
picture do you like?

Do

Build a church
with blocks.

What will you use
to decorate your
church?

Pray

Dear God,
thank You
for my beautiful
church where I can
hear about You.
Amen.

Now the LORD said to Solomon, "Keep all
My commandments. Walk in them. Then
I will establish My word with you, which I
spoke to David your father. And I will dwell
among the children of Israel. I will not leave
My people Israel."

So Solomon built the house. He finished
it. He lined the walls of the house on the
inside with boards of cedar. He overlaid
the inside of the house with pure gold.
Then all the house was finished.

Around all the walls he carved figures
of cherubim and palm trees and open
flowers. Even the floor of the house he
overlaid with gold. It took Solomon seven
years to build the house of the LORD.

Jonah

Jonah 1–4

The word of the LORD came to Jonah. He said, "Arise, go to Nineveh. Call out against it. For their evil has come up before Me."

But Jonah rose to flee from the LORD. He found a ship. He went on board to go away from the LORD.

But the LORD sent a great wind upon the sea. Then the sailors were afraid. Each cried out to his god. But Jonah had gone down into the inner part of the ship. He was fast asleep.

So the captain came and said to Jonah, "What do you mean, you sleeper? Arise, call out to your god!"

The sailors all said to Jonah, "Tell us on whose account this evil has come upon us."

He said to them, "I am a Hebrew. I fear the LORD, the God of heaven. He made the sea and the dry land."

The men knew he was fleeing from the LORD, because he had told them so.

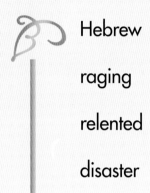

Hebrew

raging

relented

disaster

Ask

What did God want Jonah to tell the people of Nineveh?

What happened when Jonah tried to run away and hide from God?

Do

Tear a large sheet of construction paper into the shape of a big fish. Use an oval or circle for the body. Use a triangle for a fin.

On the fish print "God saves me."

Pray

Dear God,
I do not always obey You. Please forgive my sins. Help me to tell other people that You love them so much You died on the cross to save them from their sins. Amen.

Then the men were afraid. They said to Jonah, "What shall we do to you, that the sea may quiet down for us?"

Jonah said to them, "Pick me up. Hurl me into the sea. Then the sea will quiet down."

They called out to the LORD, "O LORD, let us not die for this man's life." So they picked up Jonah. They threw him into the sea.

The sea stopped its raging. Then the men feared the LORD.

And the LORD sent a great fish to swallow up Jonah. And Jonah was in the belly of the fish three days and three nights. Then Jonah prayed to the LORD his God from the belly of the fish. And the LORD spoke to the fish. It vomited Jonah out upon the dry land.

Then the LORD said, "Arise, go to Nineveh. Call out against it the message that I tell you."

So Jonah went to Nineveh. He called out, "Yet forty days, and Nineveh shall be overthrown!" And the people of Nineveh believed God.

God saw that the people of Nineveh turned from their evil way. God relented of the disaster that He had said He would do to them. He did not do it.

King Hezekiah Prays

2 Kings 18–19

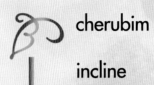

cherubim

incline

A king of Assyria came up against all the strong cities of Judah. He took them. And then his messenger went up to Jerusalem.

And the messenger said to the people of Jerusalem, "Do you think that words are power for war? In whom do you now trust? Why have you rebelled against me? Do not listen to King Hezekiah. He misleads you by saying, 'The LORD will deliver us.'"

But the people were silent. They answered him not a word.

Hezekiah received a letter from the hand of the Assyrian messengers. He read it. Then Hezekiah went up to the house of the LORD.

Hezekiah spread the letter out before the LORD. He prayed and said: "O LORD, the God of Israel, You are on a throne above the cherubim. You are the God, You alone, of all the kingdoms of the earth. You have made heaven and earth.

145

Ask

When the soldiers came, what did King Hezekiah ask God?

How did God answer King Hezekiah's prayer?

How has God answered one of your prayers?

Do

Hold up three fingers. Tell the three ways God answers prayers.

God can say *yes*, *no*, or *wait*.

Pray

Dear God,
I am glad You hear me when I pray. Thank You for taking care of me. Thank You for keeping me safe. Thank You for saving me by sending Jesus to be my Savior. Amen.

"Incline Your ear, O LORD. Hear me. Open Your eyes, O LORD. See me. Save us, please, from his hand. Then all the kingdoms of the earth may know that You, O LORD, are God alone."

Then Isaiah sent a message to Hezekiah. He said, "Thus says the LORD, the God of Israel: Your prayer to Me I have heard. This is the word that the LORD has spoken about their king:

"Whom have you mocked?

Against whom have you raised
   your voice and lifted your eyes
   to the heights?

Against the Holy One of Israel!

Because you have spoken against Me,
   I will put My hook in your nose
   and My bit in your mouth.

And I will turn you back on the way
   by which you came."

And that night the angel of the LORD went out. He struck down 185,000 in the camp of the enemy. Then the king of Assyria went home.

God Provides for Elijah

1 Kings 16–17

King Ahab was more evil than all the kings that came before him. He worshiped a false god named *Baal*.

The prophet Elijah went to King Ahab. Elijah warned the king, "God says there will be no rain for years."

Then the LORD told Elijah, "Go away from here. Hide by the brook east of the Jordan River. And drink from the brook. I told the ravens to feed you."

Elijah went. The ravens brought him bread and meat. He drank from the brook. After a while, the brook dried up.

Then the LORD said, "Arise! Go to live in Zarephath. I told a widow there to feed you."

Elijah went to the city gate. He saw a widow gathering sticks. He called to her, "Bring me a little water. I would like a drink." As she was going for water, Elijah also asked for bread.

Baal

prophet

brook

ravens

She said, "I have only a handful of flour in a jar and a little oil in a jug. I am gathering sticks so I can make bread. My son and I will eat it. Then we will die."

Elijah said, "Do not be afraid. Go and make bread. First, make me a little bread. Bring it to me. After that, make something for yourself and your son. The LORD says, 'The jar of flour shall not run out. The jug of oil will not be empty, until the day I send rain to the earth.'"

The widow did as Elijah said. They ate for many days. The jar of flour did not run out. The jug of oil did not run out.

After this, the woman's son became ill and died. The woman said to Elijah, "What did I do wrong? Did my sin cause my son to die?"

Elijah said, "Give me your son." He took the boy up to his own bed. Elijah prayed, "O LORD my God, let this child come back to life."

The LORD listened to the voice of Elijah. The child's life came into him again. Elijah brought the child to his mother. Elijah said, "See, your son lives."

The woman said, "Now I know that you are a man of God. Now I know that God's word that you speak is true."

Ask

Who kept Elijah safe from the mean king?

How did God give Elijah food and water?

How did God help Elijah take care of the woman and her son?

Do

When you buckle your seat belt, ask God to keep you safe.

When you unbuckle your seat belt, thank God for His care.

Pray

Dear God,
You love me so much! Thank You for my food. Thank You for the people who love me and take care of me. Thank You for forgiving my sins for Jesus' sake. Amen.

Elijah and the Prophets of Baal

Baal

troublemaker

sacrifice

trench

1 Kings 18

King Ahab met Elijah. "Is it you, you troublemaker?" he asked.

Elijah said, "I am not a troublemaker. You are. You do not follow the LORD. Tell the people and prophets of your gods to come to Mount Carmel."

When the people gathered, Elijah told them, "If the LORD is God, follow Him. But if Baal is God, then follow him."

Then Elijah said, "Give us two bulls. Baal's prophets can prepare one. I will prepare the other. Call on your god. I will call on the LORD God. The true God will light the fire."

The people thought it was a good plan. The prophets of Baal prepared their sacrifice.

Ask

What did Elijah build?

What happened when the people prayed to the pretend god Baal?

How did God show He was the one true God?

Do

The one true God is Father, Son, and Holy Spirit.

Hold up three fingers. Then hold up one finger. Say, "The true God is three in one."

Pray

Dear Lord, You are the true God! Help me praise and thank You every day. Help me tell others about Your love and forgiveness because of Jesus. Amen.

The prophets called on Baal from morning until noon. Nothing happened. No one answered.

Then Elijah took twelve stones. He built an altar to the LORD. He made a trench around the altar. He put the wood in order. He sacrificed the bull. Three times Elijah told the people to pour water on the altar. The water filled the trench.

Elijah prayed, "O LORD, let the people know that You are God. Let them know that You have turned their hearts back to You."

Then the LORD sent fire. It burned up the sacrifice, the wood, the stones, and even the dust. It licked up the water.

The people saw this. They fell on their faces. They said, "The LORD, He is God!"

Then Elijah and the people punished Baal's prophets.

In a little while, the heavens grew black with clouds. Then there was a great rain.

Naaman and Elisha

2 Kings 5

Naaman lived in Syria. He was a leader in the king's army. He was a man of valor. But he was a leper.

A little servant girl also lived in Syria. She was from Israel. She worked for Naaman's wife. She told Naaman's wife, "My lord should go to Samaria! God's prophet there would cure his leprosy."

Naaman told the king what the girl had said. The king replied, "Go! I will send a letter to the king of Israel."

Naaman got ready to go. He took silver, gold, and ten changes of clothing. He took a letter from his king to the king of Israel. The letter said, "I send Naaman my servant to you. Please cure his leprosy."

valor

leper

When the king read the letter, he was angry. He tore his clothes. He said, "Am I God? Can I kill and make alive? Can I cure a man of leprosy? This king wants to fight with me."

Elisha heard that the king of Israel was angry. He sent the king a message that said, "Send Naaman to me. Then he will know God's prophet is here."

Naaman took his horses and chariots to Elisha's house. He stood at the door. Elisha sent out a servant with a message. The servant said, "Go and wash seven times in the Jordan River. Then your flesh shall heal. You shall be clean."

Naaman was angry. He went away. He said, "I thought Elisha would come. I thought he would call on the LORD his God. I thought he would wave his hand and cure me. The rivers of my country are better than all the waters of Israel!"

Naaman's servants said, "The prophet spoke great words. Do what he said, 'Wash, and be clean'!"

Naaman went to the Jordan River. He dipped in it seven times. His skin was like the skin of a little child. He was clean.

Ask
What problem did Naaman have?

How did God use the little girl and Elisha to help Naaman?

Who helps you learn about Jesus?

Do
Draw pictures of people who help you when you are sick.

Thank God for these people.

Pray
Dear God,
You used a little girl and Elisha to lead Naaman to You. Thank You for the people who tell me about You. Thank You for washing away my sins and making me Your child. Amen.

The Three Men in the Fiery Furnace

Daniel 3

In Babylon King Nebuchadnezzar made an image of gold. He had the officials come to see the image. The officials were told, "You are commanded, O peoples! When you hear music, you are to fall down. Worship the golden image. And whoever does not fall down and worship shall be cast into a burning fiery furnace."

Some people said, "There are certain Judeans whom you have chosen for the work of Babylon: Shadrach, Meshach, and Abednego. These men, O king, pay no attention to you. They do not serve your gods. They do not worship the golden image that you have set up."

The king was very angry. He commanded that the three men be brought. He said to them, "Is it true that you do not serve my gods? You do not worship the golden image?"

They said, "Our God will deliver us out of your hand, O king. But if not, be it known to you that we will not serve your gods."

Ask

What are the names of the three men who did not bow down to the golden image?

Who saved the three friends?

Who saves you?

Do

Use blocks to build a community.

With a toy car, pretend to drive to all the places you made.

Say, "The true God is with me wherever I go."

Pray

Dear God, thank You for always taking care of me. I know You are the God who saves because You sent Jesus to be my Savior. Help me not to be afraid. Help me to trust in You. Amen.

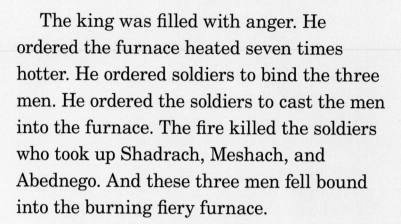

The king was filled with anger. He ordered the furnace heated seven times hotter. He ordered soldiers to bind the three men. He ordered the soldiers to cast the men into the furnace. The fire killed the soldiers who took up Shadrach, Meshach, and Abednego. And these three men fell bound into the burning fiery furnace.

Then the king declared, "Did we not cast three men bound into the fire?"

People said to the king, "True, O king."

He said, "But I see four men unbound. They are walking in the fire. They are not hurt. The fourth one is like a son of the gods."

Then the king came near to the furnace. He declared, "Servants of the Most High God, come out!"

Then the three men came out from the fire. The fire did not have any power over the bodies of those men.

The king said, "Blessed is your God. He has sent His angel. He has delivered His servants, who trusted in Him."

Daniel in the Lions' Den

Daniel 6

Daniel was different. A good spirit was in him. And the king planned to set Daniel over the whole kingdom.

Then the other officials came to the king. They said, "O King Darius, live forever! The king should establish a law. Whoever prays to any god or man, except to you, O king, shall be cast into the den of lions. Now, O king, sign the law. Then it cannot be changed." King Darius signed the law.

When Daniel knew that the law had been signed, he went to his house. He got down on his knees three times a day. He prayed and gave thanks before his God, as he had done before.

Then these men found Daniel praying before his God. They said, "Daniel is one of the exiles from Judah. He does not listen to you, O king. He prays three times a day."

Then the king was very upset. He set his mind to deliver Daniel.

exiles

fasting

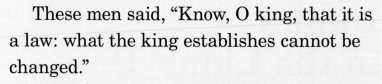

Ask

Look at the picture. Where is Daniel?

What does the king wonder?

Whom does God send to protect Daniel?

Do

Make different animal sounds.

Which animals frighten you?

Remember God sends His angels to watch over you.

Pray

Dear Jesus, thank You for loving me. Thank You for protecting me. Help me remember that You are the one true God. Help me trust in You. Help me not to be afraid. Amen.

These men said, "Know, O king, that it is a law: what the king establishes cannot be changed."

Then Daniel was brought and cast into the den of lions. The king declared to Daniel, "May your God, whom you serve continually, deliver you!"

A stone was brought and laid on the mouth of the den. The king sealed it. Then the king went to his palace. He spent the night fasting. Sleep fled from him.

Then, at break of day, the king went quickly to the den of lions. He cried out, "O Daniel, servant of the living God! Has your God been able to deliver you?"

Then Daniel said, "O king, live forever! My God sent His angel. He shut the lions' mouths. They have not harmed me." Then the king was very glad. He commanded that Daniel be taken up out of the den. No kind of harm was found on him, because he had trusted in his God.

Then those men who had said bad things about Daniel were cast into the den of lions. Before they reached the bottom of the den, the lions overpowered them. They broke all their bones in pieces.

160

Waiting for God's Messenger

wearied

covenant

righteousness

stall

Malachi 2–4

This is the word of the Lord to Israel by Malachi. He wrote the last book of the Old Testament. He wrote:

You have wearied the LORD with your words. But you say, "How have we wearied Him?" By saying, "Everyone who does evil is good in the sight of the LORD. He delights in them." Or you ask, 'Where is the God of justice?'"

The LORD said: "Behold, I send My messenger. He will prepare the way before Me. And the Lord whom you seek will suddenly come to His temple.

"He is the messenger of the covenant in whom you delight. Behold, He is coming, says the LORD of hosts."

The LORD said to those who honored His name: "For you who fear My name, the sun of righteousness shall rise with healing in its wings. You shall go out leaping joyfully like calves from the stall.

"Behold, I will send you Elijah the prophet. He will come before the great and awesome day of the LORD comes. And he will turn the hearts of fathers to their children. He will turn the hearts of children to their fathers."

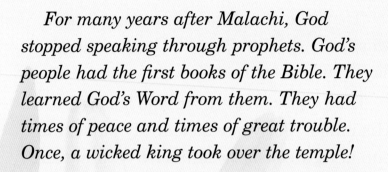

Ask

The Lord told Malachi that He would send a messenger. What is a messenger?

What will the messenger do?

Do

Malachi says that the people will have to wait for God's messenger. While they wait, they hope.

You can be a messenger. Tell someone you will write them a note. Then write it and deliver it.

Pray

Dear Jesus, as I wait for You to come again, help me to fear, love, and trust in You above all things now and forever. Amen.

For many years after Malachi, God stopped speaking through prophets. God's people had the first books of the Bible. They learned God's Word from them. They had times of peace and times of great trouble. Once, a wicked king took over the temple!

But God had promised to send a special messenger. God's promise gave the people hope. It would come true in God's time. That is what the next part of the Bible is all about. ❋

The New Testament

The Birth of John Foretold

Luke 1

In the days of Herod, king of Judea, there was a priest named Zechariah. And he had a wife from the daughters of Aaron. Her name was Elizabeth. They were both righteous before God. They kept all the commandments of the Lord. But they had no child. For they were both old.

Now Zechariah was serving as priest before God. He was chosen to enter the temple of the Lord. There he burned incense. A large group of people were praying outside. And there appeared to him an angel of the Lord. The angel stood on the right side of the altar. And Zechariah was afraid when he saw him.

But the angel said, "Do not be afraid. Your prayer has been heard. Your wife Elizabeth will have a son. You shall call his name *John*. And you will have joy. For he will be great before the Lord. He will be filled with the Holy Spirit. And he will turn many of the children of Israel to the Lord their God."

incense

appeared

vision

signs

conceived

Ask

Who surprised Zechariah in the temple?

What good news did he tell Zechariah?

What happened to Zechariah?

Do

Try using your hands to talk. Give someone a message using signs.

How would you say, "I saw an angel"?

Pray

Heavenly Father, thank You for sending Your angel to Zechariah with good news. Help me believe the Good News that Jesus is my Savior. Amen.

Zechariah said, "How shall I know this? For I am an old man. My wife is old too."

And the angel said, "I am Gabriel. I stand in the presence of God. I bring you this good news. And behold, you will not be able to speak until the day that these things take place. For you did not believe my words."

The people were waiting for Zechariah. They were wondering at his delay in the temple. And when he came out, he was not able to speak to them. And they knew that he had seen a vision in the temple. And he kept making signs to them. For he could not talk.

And when his time of service was ended, he went home.

Soon Elizabeth conceived. She said, "The Lord has done this for me." ✶

The Birth of Jesus Foretold

Luke 1

The angel Gabriel was sent from God to a city of Galilee. The city was named Nazareth. Gabriel came to a virgin. She was promised to marry a man whose name was Joseph. He was of the house of David. The virgin's name was Mary.

The angel said, "Greetings, O favored one. The Lord is with you!"

But Mary was troubled at the saying. She did not understand what sort of greeting this might be.

The angel said to her, "Do not be afraid, Mary. For you have found favor with God. Behold! You will conceive and have a Son. And you shall call His name *Jesus*. He will be great. He will be called the Son of the Most High. And the Lord God will give Him the throne. He will rule forever. His kingdom will never end."

virgin

favored

conceive

Mary said to the angel, "How will this be, since I am a virgin?"

The angel said, "The Holy Spirit will come upon you. The power of the Most High will do this. So the child will be called holy—the Son of God.

"Behold! Your relative Elizabeth, who is old, is also going to have a baby. Nothing will be impossible with God."

Mary said, "Behold! I am the servant of the Lord. Let it be done according to your word."

Then the angel left. ★

Ask

What did the angel say to Mary?
What did Mary say to the angel?

Do

Mary was the mother of Jesus. She lived in Nazareth.

What is your mother's name? Find out where she lived when you were born.

Pray

Heavenly Father, You chose Mary to be the mother of Jesus, my Savior. Thank You for choosing me to be Your child. Amen.

Mary Visits Elizabeth

fruit of your womb

magnifies

Luke 1

The angel Gabriel told Mary, "Behold! You will have a Son. You shall call His name *Jesus*."

The angel also told her, "Your relative Elizabeth, who is old, is also going to have a baby."

In those days, Mary went quickly to the hill country. She came to a town in Judah. And she entered the house of Zechariah. She greeted Elizabeth. And Elizabeth heard Mary's greeting. Then the baby leaped in Elizabeth's womb!

And Elizabeth was filled with the Holy Spirit. She said with a loud cry, "Blessed are you! And blessed is the fruit of your womb. Behold! The sound of your greeting came to my ears. Then the baby in my womb leaped for joy."

And Mary said,

"My soul magnifies the Lord.

My spirit rejoices in God my Savior. For He has looked on me.

Behold! All people will call me blessed.

Ask

What did the baby inside Elizabeth do when he heard Mary's voice?

Was Mary happy to be the mother of Jesus?

Do

Mary said her soul magnified the Lord. She praised God with happy words.

You can magnify the Lord too. Use happy words to tell what God has done for you.

Pray

Heavenly Father, Mary praised You with happy words. I praise You too, for You have done great things for me. You sent Jesus to be my Savior. Amen.

The mighty God has done great things for me.

Holy is His name.

He gives mercy to those who trust in Him.

He has shown strength with His arm.

He has scattered the proud.

He has brought down the mighty.

He has lifted up the humble.

He has filled the hungry with good things.

He has sent away the rich with nothing.

He has helped His children."

Mary stayed with Elizabeth about three months. Then she went home.

The Birth of John

Luke 1

The time came. Elizabeth gave birth to a son. Her neighbors and relatives heard about the Lord's mercy to her. On the eighth day they came to rejoice.

They would have called the baby Zechariah. That was his father's name. But his mother said, "No. He shall be called *John.*"

They said to her, "None of your relatives is called by this name." Then they made signs to Zechariah. He still could not speak. They asked him what he wanted the baby to be called.

Zechariah asked for a writing tablet. He wrote, "His name is John." And they all wondered.

Right away Zechariah spoke. He blessed God.

All these things were talked about through all the hill country. Everyone who heard them said, "What will this child be?"

mercy

prophesied

redeemed

prophets

salvation

Ask

When the baby was born, who came to rejoice with Zechariah and Elizabeth?

What did Zechariah and Elizabeth name the baby?

What did Zechariah say about the baby?

Do

God's people still sing Zechariah's happy words.

Make up a happy song about how God has blessed your family.

Pray

Heavenly Father, You sent John to tell people that Jesus was coming to forgive their sins. Thank You for grown-up people who tell me that Jesus loves me and can forgive the wrong things I think or say or do. Amen.

Zechariah was filled with the Holy Spirit. He prophesied, saying,

"Blessed be the Lord God.

He has visited His people.

He has redeemed His people.

He spoke by the mouth of His holy prophets.

He said we should be saved from our enemies.

Then we, being saved, might serve Him without fear.

And you, child, will be called the prophet of the Most High.

You will go before the Lord. You will prepare His ways.

You will make known salvation to His people.

You will tell about the forgiveness of sins.

For the tender mercy of our God will give light to those who sit in darkness.

God will guide our feet in the way of peace."

After this John grew. He became strong in spirit. And when he was older, he lived in the wilderness. ★

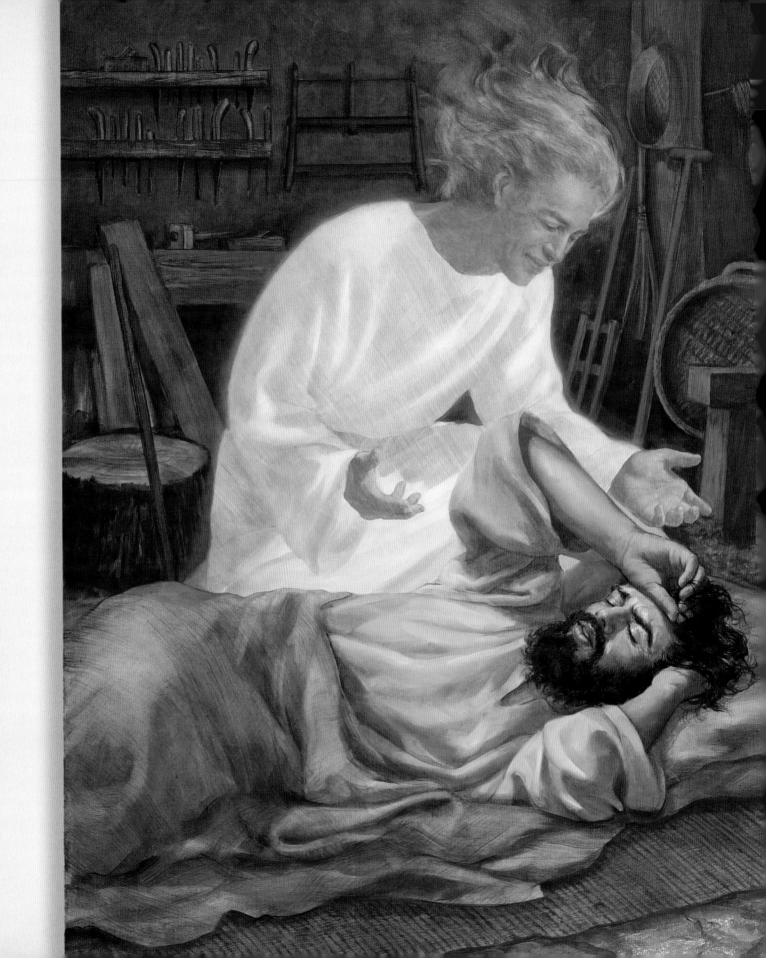

An Angel Visits Joseph

Matthew 1

Long, long ago, God told people about His promise to send a Savior. But before Jesus came to earth as a baby, God had to help people get ready.

Now the birth of Jesus Christ took place in this way. Mary and Joseph were planning to be married. They were betrothed. Before they came together, Mary was found to be with child from the Holy Spirit.

Joseph was a just man. He thought he would divorce Mary quietly. But as he thought about these things, an angel of the Lord came to him in a dream.

The angel said, "Joseph, son of David, do not be afraid. You can take Mary as your wife. The baby is from the Holy Spirit. She will have a Son. You shall call His name *Jesus*. He will save His people from their sins."

betrothed

divorce

prophet

Immanuel

commanded

181

Ask

What problem did Joseph have?

What did the angel tell Joseph?

What name would Joseph give the baby?

Do

Make an angel from an upside-down white paper cup. Use a marker to give the angel a face.

Have the angel repeat the words spoken to Joseph.

Pray

Dear God, I am so glad to know the truth that Jesus is my Immanuel. Amen.

Then Joseph knew Mary was telling the truth.

All this took place just as the Lord had spoken many years before. The prophet Isaiah said:

"Behold, the virgin shall conceive. She will have a Son. They shall call His name *Immanuel*."

Immanuel means "God with us."

Joseph woke up from his sleep. He did what the angel of the Lord commanded him to do. He took Mary as his wife. Later, when the baby was born, Joseph called His name *Jesus*. ★

Immanuel

The Birth of Jesus

Luke 2

In those days the Roman ruler told all the people to register for a census. All went to be registered, each to his own town. Joseph also went to Bethlehem. He took Mary.

While they were there, the time came for her to give birth. She gave birth to her first child, a Son. She wrapped Him in cloths. She placed Him in a manger. For there was no room for them in the inn.

Not far away shepherds were in the field. They were watching their flock by night. An angel appeared. The glory of the Lord shone around them. They were filled with fear.

The angel said, "Fear not. For behold! I bring you good news of a great joy for all people. To you is born this day a Savior. He is Christ the Lord. You will find a baby wrapped in cloths and lying in a manger."

Suddenly there were many angels. They praised God and said,

"Glory to God in the highest,
and peace on earth!"

The angels went away. Then the shepherds said, "Let us go and see this thing."

register

census

manger

treasured

devout

They went quickly. They found Mary and Joseph and the baby in a manger. When they saw it, they told others about this child. And all who heard it wondered at what the shepherds told them. Mary treasured up all these things in her heart.

At the end of eight days, the baby was called *Jesus*. This was the name given to Him by the angel before He was born.

When the time came, Joseph and Mary brought Jesus to the temple in Jerusalem.

A man in Jerusalem named Simeon was righteous and devout. The Holy Spirit revealed to him that he would not die before he had seen the Lord's Christ. Simeon was at the temple and took the baby in his arms. He blessed God and said,

"Lord, now let me go in peace.
My eyes have seen Your salvation.

He is a light to the Gentiles,
and a glory to Your people."

His father and mother wondered at what Simeon said about Jesus. Simeon blessed them.

Ask

Where was Jesus born?

Who told the shepherds the good news about the baby?

Do

Use play dough and boxes to make a stable, manger, Mary, Joseph, and baby Jesus.

Pray

Dear Jesus, I love to hear the story of Your birth. Glory to God! You came to be my Savior. Amen.

There was a prophetess, Anna. She was old and a widow. She did not leave the temple.

She worshiped God by fasting and praying night and day. She came and gave thanks to God. She spoke of Jesus to all.

When they had done all the Law said to do, Mary and Joseph went back to Nazareth.

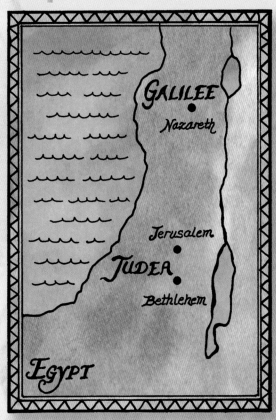

GALILEE

Nazareth

Jerusalem

JUDEA

Bethlehem

EGYPT

The Visit of the Wise Men

Matthew 2

After Jesus was born, Wise Men from the east came to Jerusalem. They asked King Herod, "Where is He who has been born King of the Jews? We saw His star and have come to worship Him."

When King Herod heard this, he was worried. He met with the chief priests and scribes. He asked them where the Christ was to be born.

They told him, "In Bethlehem. For that is written by the prophet."

Then Herod met secretly with the Wise Men. He asked them when the star had appeared. Then he sent them to Bethlehem. He said, "Go and search for the child. When you have found Him, tell me. I want to come and worship Him."

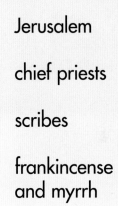

Jerusalem

chief priests

scribes

frankincense and myrrh

The Wise Men went on their way. Behold, the star went before them. It rested over the place where the child was. When they saw the star, they rejoiced.

They went into the house and saw the child with Mary, His mother. They knelt down and worshiped Jesus. Then they opened their treasures. They offered Him gifts of gold and frankincense and myrrh. And they were warned in a dream not to return to Herod. So they returned to their own country another way.

An angel of the Lord came to Joseph in a dream. The angel said, "Get up, and take the child and His mother. Flee to Egypt. Stay there until I tell you. For King Herod is about to search for the child, to destroy Him."

That night, Joseph took the child and His mother to Egypt. They stayed there until the death of King Herod. ★

Ask

What did God use to lead the Wise Men to Jesus?

How did God keep Jesus safe?

Do

Draw a Bible-times house and stars in the dark sky.

Draw one special star over the house.

Pray

Heavenly Father, thank You for leading the Wise Men to see and worship Jesus. Lead me to see Jesus and worship Him as my Savior. Amen.

The Boy Jesus in the Temple

Passover Feast

My Father's house

stature

Luke 2

Jesus grew and became strong. He became wise. The favor of God was upon Him.

Jesus grew up in a little town called Nazareth. Each year, Joseph and Mary went to Jerusalem for the Passover Feast. When Jesus was twelve, He went too.

When the feast was ended, Jesus stayed behind. His parents did not know it.

At the end of a day's walk, Jesus' parents looked for Him. But they did not find Him! So Joseph and Mary went back to Jerusalem.

After three days, they found Jesus.

Ask

What did Jesus and His parents do in Jerusalem?

Do

While Jesus grew up, He took time to hear God's Word. You are growing too.

Measure how tall you are. Then tell where you hear God's Word.

Pray

Dear Jesus, as a boy You loved to go to the temple and hear God's Word. As I grow, help me to love God's Word too. I want to learn more about You. Amen.

Jesus was in the temple with the teachers. He was listening and asking questions. Those who heard Jesus talk were amazed.

When His parents saw Jesus, they were surprised. His mother said, "Son, why have You done this? Your father and I have been sad. We searched for You."

Jesus said, "Why were you looking for Me? Did you not know that I must be in My Father's house?"

Mary and Joseph did not understand.

Then it was time to go back home. Jesus went with them to Nazareth. He obeyed Joseph and Mary.

Jesus grew in wisdom and in stature. He grew in favor with God and man. ★

Isaiah 9:6

194

John Prepares the Way of the Lord

Matthew 3; Luke 3

John the Baptist came preaching in the wilderness. He said, "Repent! The kingdom of heaven is near." Years before, the prophet Isaiah spoke about John. He said,

> "The voice of one shouting in the wilderness,
>
> 'Prepare the way of the Lord.' "

John wore clothing of camel's hair. He wore a leather belt. And his food was locusts and wild honey.

Some people who were sorry for their sins came to John. They were baptized by him in the river Jordan.

John said to others, "Do things that show you repent of your sins."

The crowds asked him, "What shall we do?"

John said, "Whoever has two shirts is to share with him who has none. Whoever has food is to share too."

wilderness

repent

kingdom of heaven

baptized

Tax collectors also came to be baptized. They said to John, "Teacher, what shall we do?"

He said, "Take no more money than is right for you to take."

Soldiers also asked him, "What shall we do?"

And John said, "Do not take people's money away. Be happy with your wages."

People were wondering, "Might John be the Christ?"

But John said, "I baptize you with water for repentance. But one is coming after me. He is mightier than I am. He will baptize you with the Holy Spirit and with fire."

So with many other words John preached good news to the people.

Ask

What did John wear?
What did John eat?
What did John say and do?

Do

Make a model of John preaching in the wilderness.

Use chenille wires to make a body and scraps of cloth to make clothing.

Pray

Dear Jesus, I think and say and do mean things. I need to repent. Teach me to come to You and say that I am sorry. Amen.

The Baptism of Jesus

righteousness

beloved

John 1; Matthew 3

These things took place in Bethany across the Jordan River. That is where John was baptizing.

John saw Jesus coming toward him. John said, "Behold, the Lamb of God. He takes away the sin of the world! This is the one who comes after me. This is why I came baptizing with water, that He might be revealed to Israel."

Jesus came to the Jordan River. He wanted to be baptized by John.

John tried to stop Jesus. He said, "I need to be baptized by You. Why do You come to me?"

Jesus said, "Let it be so now. Baptize Me to fulfill all righteousness." John said he would.

Ask

What did Jesus ask John to do?

What happened after Jesus came up from the water?

Do

Use water to wash something clean.

How is water used in Baptism?

Pray

Dear Jesus, give me eyes of faith to see that You are God's beloved Son. Amen.

After Jesus was baptized, He went up from the water. And behold! The heavens were opened. Jesus saw the Spirit of God coming down like a dove. The dove came to rest on Him. And behold! A voice from heaven said, "This is My beloved Son. With Him I am well pleased."

Later, John said to others, "I saw the Spirit come down from heaven like a dove. The Spirit remained on Jesus. I have seen this. I have borne witness that this is the Son of God."

The Temptation of Jesus

Matthew 4; Mark 1; Luke 4

Jesus was led into the wilderness by the Holy Spirit. There He would be tempted by the devil. And He was with the wild animals.

Jesus did not eat for forty days and forty nights. He was hungry. And the devil said, "If You are the Son of God, command these stones to become bread." But Jesus said, "It is written,

" 'Man shall not live by bread alone,
but by every word that comes
from God.' "

Then the devil took Jesus to the holy city. He set Him on the top of the temple. And the devil said, "If You are the Son of God, throw Yourself down. It is written,

" 'He will command His angels to
protect You.' "

Jesus said, "It is written, 'You shall not test the Lord your God.' "

tempted

ministering

worship

Again, the devil took Jesus to a very high mountain. He showed Jesus all the kingdoms of the world and their glory.

And the devil said, "I will give You all this, if You will worship me."

Then Jesus said to him, "Be gone, Satan! For it is written,

" 'You shall worship the Lord your God. Serve only Him.' "

Then the devil left. And behold! Angels came to help Jesus.

And Jesus returned in the power of the Spirit to Galilee. And a report about Him went out throughout the country. And He taught in their places of prayer. Everyone spoke well of Him.

Ask
The devil is tricky. What did the devil want Jesus to do?

Do
Jesus could repeat Bible words that He knew.
What Bible words do you know? Repeat them.

Pray
Dear Jesus, thank You for saying "no" to the devil when he tempted You. Lead me not into temptation, but deliver me from evil. Amen.

Jesus Calls Disciples

Rabbi

Messiah

Christ

John 1

After Jesus was baptized, two of John's disciples followed Jesus. He said to them, "What are you seeking?"

They said, "Rabbi, where are You staying?"

He said, "Come and you will see."

So they stayed with Him that day. One of them was Andrew. Andrew went and found his brother Simon Peter. He said, "We have found the Messiah!" (This means "Christ.") He brought Simon Peter to Jesus.

The next day Jesus wanted to go to Galilee. He met Philip, who was from the same city as Andrew and Peter. Jesus said to Philip, "Follow Me."

So Philip found Nathanael. He said to him, "We have found Him! Moses in the Law and also the prophets wrote about Him. He is Jesus of Nazareth, the son of Joseph."

Nathanael said to Philip, "Can anything good come out of Nazareth?"

Ask

What did Jesus ask Philip to do?

Whom did Philip go tell?

What did Philip tell Nathanael about Jesus?

Do

Open your hands like an open Bible. Say, "Lord, to whom shall we go? You have the words of eternal life." John 6:68

Pray

Dear Jesus, thank You for calling me to be Your child. Amen.

Philip said to him, "Come and see."

Jesus saw Nathanael coming toward Him. He said of him, "Behold, an Israelite indeed! In him there is no lie!"

Nathanael said to Him, "How do You know me?"

Jesus said, "Before Philip called you, when you were under the fig tree, I saw you."

Nathanael said, "Rabbi, You are the Son of God! You are the King of Israel!"

Jesus said, "Do you believe because I said this? You will see greater things than these. Truly, truly, I say to you, you will see heaven opened."

Jesus Changes Water into Wine

John 2

On the third day there was a wedding. It was at Cana in Galilee. The mother of Jesus was there. Jesus also was invited to the wedding with His disciples.

But the wine ran out. The mother of Jesus said to Him, "They have no wine."

And Jesus said to her, "Woman, what does this have to do with Me? My hour has not yet come."

His mother said to the servants, "Do whatever He tells you."

Now there were six stone water jars there for washing. Each jar held twenty or thirty gallons. Jesus said to the servants, "Fill the jars with water." And they filled them up to the brim. And He said to them, "Now draw some out. Take it to the master of the feast." So they took it.

My hour

gallons

brim

draw

manifested

Then the master of the feast tasted the water now become wine. He did not know where it came from. (The servants who had drawn the water knew.) The master of the feast called the bridegroom. He said to him, "Everyone serves the good wine first. When people have drunk freely, then they serve the poor wine. But you have kept the good wine until now."

Jesus did this first sign at Cana in Galilee. And He manifested His glory. And His disciples believed in Him.

After this Jesus went down to Capernaum. He went with His mother and His brothers and His disciples. And they stayed there a few days.

Ask

Where did Jesus go with His disciples?
What miracle did Jesus do?

Do

Draw things you like to eat and drink.
Talk about how God takes care of you.

Pray

Dear Jesus, thank You for the Bible where You show me that You are God. You are the Savior of all people. Amen.

The Disciples Follow Jesus

repent

kingdom
of heaven

casting

pressing in

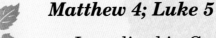

Matthew 4; Luke 5

Jesus lived in Capernaum by the sea. So what was spoken by the prophet Isaiah was fulfilled:

"The way of the sea, beyond the Jordan, Galilee of the Gentiles—

the people dwelling in darkness have seen a great light.

For those dwelling in the shadow of death,

on them a light has dawned."

From that time Jesus began to preach. He said, "Repent! For the kingdom of heaven is near."

Jesus walked by the Sea of Galilee. He saw two brothers. He saw Simon Peter and Andrew his brother. They were casting a net into the sea. For they were fishermen. He said to them, "Follow Me. I will make you fishers of men."

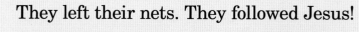

Ask

What jobs do the men have?

Who is calling the men to do something new?

What will be their new job?

Do

Draw a picture of the people in your family who follow (believe in) Jesus.

Pray

Thank You, Jesus, for sending pastors and church workers to tell people about Your love and forgiveness. Help me share Your love with others too. Amen.

They left their nets. They followed Jesus!

Going on from there Jesus saw two other brothers. He saw James and John. They were in the boat with their father. Jesus called them. Right away they left the boat and their father. They followed Jesus!

Once, the crowd was pressing in on Jesus. They wanted to hear the Word of God.

Jesus was standing by the lake. He saw two boats there. He got into one of the boats, which was Simon's. He asked Simon to go out a little from the land. Jesus sat down and taught the people from the boat.

Later, Jesus said to Simon, "Put the boat out into the deep water. Let down your nets for a catch."

And Simon said, "Master, we worked all night! We caught nothing! But at Your word I will let down the nets."

When they had done this, they caught a large number of fish. They filled two boats. They began to sink!

But when Simon Peter saw it, he fell
down at Jesus' knees. He said, "Depart
from me. For I am a sinful man, O Lord."
For he and all who were with him
were astonished at the catch of fish
that they had taken.

Jesus said to Simon, "Do not be afraid.
From now on you will be catching men."
And when they had brought their boats
to land, they left everything.
They followed Jesus!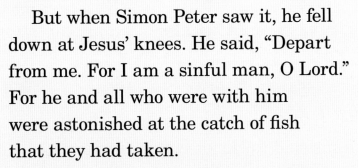

Jesus Heals a Paralyzed Man

paralytic

scribes

authority

Mark 1–2

Jesus said to His disciples, "Let us go on to the next towns. I want to preach there too."

And so Jesus walked throughout Galilee, preaching and healing.

After some days, Jesus returned to Capernaum. There He was at home. Many people gathered together. There was no more room in the house, not even at the door. He was preaching the word to them.

Some people came, bringing a paralyzed man. He was carried by four men.

The four men could not get near Jesus because of the crowd. So they removed the roof above Him. They made an opening. Then they let down the bed on which the paralyzed man lay.

Jesus saw their faith. He said to the paralytic, "Son, your sins are forgiven."

Ask

What did the four men do for the paralyzed man?

Who did not believe Jesus could forgive sins?

Can Jesus forgive sins?

What miracle did Jesus do?

Do

Jesus healed the paralyzed man so that he could use his legs.

What kinds of things can you do with your legs? Walk? Jump? Kick? Kneel? Stand?

Pray

Dear Jesus, You forgave the sins of the paralyzed man. You made him walk again so others would believe that You are the Savior. You are my Savior too. Please forgive my sins. Amen.

Now some of the scribes were sitting there. They said, "Why does this man speak like that? Only God can forgive sins."

Jesus knew they had questions. He said to them, "Why do you question these things? Which is easier, to say to the paralytic, 'Your sins are forgiven,' or to say, 'Rise, take up your bed and walk'? But that you may know that I have the authority on earth to forgive sins"—He said to the paralyzed man— "I say to you, rise! Pick up your bed, and go home."

The man rose. He picked up his bed. He went out before them all. They were all amazed. They gave God glory. They said, "We never saw anything like this!"

Jesus Calms a Storm

Mark 4

Large crowds gathered to hear Jesus. He spoke to people with special stories called parables. Many people did not understand the stories. But Jesus explained all these stories to His disciples.

perishing

rebuked

calm

One evening after Jesus had done a lot of teaching, He said, "Let us go across the water to the other side." And leaving the crowd, the disciples took Him with them in the boat. And other boats were with Him.

A great windstorm arose. The waves came into the boat. They were so high that the boat was filling with water.

Jesus was in the back of the boat, which is called the stern. He was asleep on the cushion.

The disciples woke Jesus. They said to Him, "Teacher, do You not care? We are perishing!"

He awoke and rebuked the wind. He said to the sea, "Peace! Be still!" The wind stopped. There was a great calm.

Then Jesus said to the disciples, "Why are you so afraid? Do you still have no faith?"

The disciples were filled with great fear. They said to one another, "Who is this? Even the wind and sea obey Him!"

The disciples still did not understand who Jesus was. They would still learn that He was the Messiah. They would learn that He was the Son of God. ✹

Ask

What is the scary part of the story?

What is the happy part of the story?

What miracle did Jesus do?

Do

Fold paper and make a little boat. Float the boat in a dish of water.

Act out the Bible story.

Pray

Dear Jesus, You love and care for me at all times, even during scary storms. Thank You for watching over me. Amen.

Jesus Heals Jairus's Daughter

weeping

wailing

amazed

Mark 5

Once again, a great crowd gathered about Jesus. One of the rulers of the prayer house, Jairus, came too. When Jairus saw Jesus, he fell at Jesus' feet. He said, "My little daughter is about to die. Come and lay Your hands on her. Then she will be made well and live." And Jesus went with him.

A great crowd followed Jesus.

As they walked, some people came from the ruler's house. They said, "Your daughter is dead. Why trouble the Teacher?"

But Jesus said, "Do not fear, only believe."

Then Jesus did not let anyone follow Him except Peter and James and John. They came to the house of the ruler of the prayer house. Jesus saw people weeping and wailing loudly. He said to them, "Why are you making noise and weeping? The child is not dead but sleeping."

They laughed at Jesus.

Ask

What did the ruler of the prayer house ask Jesus to do?

What happened when Jesus got to the ruler's house?

What miracle did Jesus do?

Do

The sick girl's father talked to Jesus.

You can talk to Jesus in prayer. Pray for the people you love who are sick.

Pray

Dear Jesus, thank You that I can ask You for help when I am sick. I believe that You will hear me pray. Amen.

But Jesus sent them all outside. Then He took the child's father and mother. He took the three disciples. They went with Him to the child. Taking her hand Jesus said to her, "Little girl, I say to you, arise."

Just then the girl got up. She began walking (for she was twelve years old). They were amazed. Jesus told them that no one should know this. He also told them to give her something to eat.

Jesus Walks on Water

Matthew 14

Jesus fed five thousand people beside the Sea of Galilee. He told the disciples to pick up the leftover food. They collected twelve baskets full.

Jesus made the disciples get into the boat right away and go to the other side. Jesus sent all the people home. Then He went up on the mountain to pray. When evening came, He was alone. The boat was a long way from the land. The boat was hit by the waves. For the wind was against the boat.

In the fourth watch of the night, Jesus came to the disciples walking on the sea. When they saw Him walking on the sea, they were very afraid. They said, "It is a ghost!" The disciples cried out in fear.

watch
of the night

faith

Jesus said right away, "Take heart. It is I. Do not be afraid."

And Peter said, "Lord, if it is You, tell me to come to You on the water."

Jesus said, "Come."

So Peter got out of the boat. He walked on the water and came to Jesus. But when Peter saw the wind, he was afraid. He began to sink. He cried out, "Lord, save me."

Right away Jesus reached out His hand. He took hold of Peter. He said, "O you of little faith. Why did you doubt?"

When they got into the boat, the wind stopped. Those in the boat worshiped Jesus. They said, "Truly You are the Son of God."

Ask

How did Jesus get to the boat?

What did Peter try to do?

Do

Fill a container with water. Find some items that sink or float. Put them in the water.

What happened when Peter walked on water?

Pray

Dear Jesus, Peter was in trouble and You saved him. When I am in trouble, please help and save me too. Amen.

The Transfiguration

Mark 8–9

rebuke

transfigured

radiant

beloved

Jesus began to teach the disciples that the Son of Man must suffer many things. He must be rejected by the elders and the chief priests and the scribes. He must be killed and after three days rise again. He said this plainly.

Peter took Jesus aside. He began to rebuke Him.

But Jesus rebuked Peter. He said, "You are not setting your mind on the things of God."

Six days later, Jesus took Peter and James and John with Him. He led them up a high mountain. He was transfigured before them. His clothes became radiant and very white.

At that time, Elijah and Moses appeared. They were talking with Jesus.

Ask

What happened to Jesus' clothes?

Which two men stood by Jesus?

What did the voice from the cloud say?

Do

Add glitter to play dough and make something.

Talk about how Jesus sparkled with God's glory.

Pray

Dear Jesus, thank You for washing away my sins and making me Your child. Amen.

Peter said to Jesus, "It is good that we are here. Let us make three tents. One could be for You, one for Moses, and one for Elijah." For Peter did not know what to say. Peter, James, and John were very frightened.

Then the shadow of a cloud came over them. A voice came out of the cloud. It said, "This is My beloved Son. Listen to Him."

Then, looking around, Peter, James, and John did not see anyone with them. Only Jesus was there.

They came down the mountain. And Jesus told them not to tell what they had seen, until He had risen from the dead. So Peter, James, and John kept the matter to themselves.

Jesus Heals a Blind Man

John 9

Jesus saw a man who was blind from birth. His disciples asked Him, "Rabbi, who sinned, this man or his parents, that he was born blind?"

Jesus said, "It was not that this man sinned or his parents. It is so the works of God might be shown in him. We must work the works of God who sent Me while we can. The time is coming when no one can work. As long as I am in the world, I am the light of the world."

Then Jesus made mud with spit. He put it on the man's eyes. Jesus said, "Go, wash in the pool." So the man went and washed. He came back seeing.

Some neighbors had seen the man before as a beggar. They said, "Is this the man who used to sit and beg?" Some said, "It is he." Others said, "No, but he is like him."

Rabbi

spit

beggar

Son of Man

The man who had been blind said, "I am the man."

So they said to him, "Then how were your eyes opened?"

He said, "The man called Jesus made mud. He put it on my eyes. He said, 'Go to the pool and wash.' So I went. I washed. Then I could see again."

Later Jesus found the man again. He said, "Do you believe in the Son of Man?"

He said, "Who is He, sir?"

Jesus said, "You have seen Him. It is I, the one who is speaking to you."

The man said, "Lord, I believe." And he worshiped Jesus.

Ask

What did Jesus do to help the man who was blind?

Do

Play a game of I Spy outside. Say, "I spy something God made that is (describe the color or shape of an object)."

Pray

Dear Jesus, You healed a man who was blind, and He believed in You. Thank You for faith so I can believe in You too. Amen.

The Beatitudes

Matthew 4–5

blessed

kingdom
of heaven

meek

inherit

merciful

Jesus went throughout all Galilee. He was teaching the Gospel. He was healing the people. And great crowds followed Him.

One day, Jesus went up on a mountain and sat down. His disciples came near. He taught them, saying:

"Blessed are the poor in spirit. For theirs is the kingdom of heaven.

"Blessed are those who mourn, who are sad over sin. For they shall be comforted.

"Blessed are the meek. For they shall inherit the earth.

"Blessed are those who hunger and thirst for righteousness. For they shall be satisfied.

"Blessed are the merciful. For they shall receive mercy.

"Blessed are the pure in heart. For they shall see God.

"Blessed are the peacemakers. For they shall be called sons of God.

"Blessed are those who get in trouble for doing the right thing. For theirs is the kingdom of heaven.

Ask

On the mountain, Jesus says nine beatitudes. They tell of good things or blessings that will be ours in the future.

Which beatitude is your favorite?

Do

Make up actions to the words as you say this rhyme.

> My life is full of
>   blessings that come
>   from Jesus' love.
>
> Like parents, friends
>   and neighbors, and
>   sunshine from above.
>
> When Jesus died upon
>   the cross, He took
>   my sins away.
>
> I'm blessed for sure.
>   I can rejoice and
>   be glad every day.

Pray

Dear Jesus,
when I have troubles,
let me see Your blessings.
Thank You for forgiving
me and giving me eternal
life with You.
Amen.

"Blessed are you when others say and do evil against you because of Me. Rejoice and be glad. For your reward is great in heaven."

Jesus sat and talked to His friends. He wanted them to know that the things they say about God and the things they do are important. Our words and actions show our love for God.

Jesus said to His disciples, "You are the salt of the earth. You are the light of the world."

The Sermon on the Mount

Matthew 5–6

Jesus said, "I have not come to get rid of God's Word of Law or the Prophets. I have come to keep them. Whoever keeps them and teaches them will be called great in the kingdom of heaven.

"You have heard, 'You shall not kill.' But I say that everyone who is angry with his brother will have God's judgment.

"Again you have heard, 'You shall not lie when you take an oath. Instead do what you have promised.' But I say to you, do not take an oath. Say simply 'Yes' or 'No.'

"You have heard, 'You shall love your neighbor and hate your enemy.' But I say, love your enemies. Pray for those who are mean to you, so that you may be sons of your Father who is in heaven."

Jesus wanted everyone to know how much our heavenly Father loves His children.

Law or the Prophets

kingdom of heaven

oath

spin

So Jesus talked to the people with Him about how God cares for the flowers and the birds.

Jesus said, "Do not worry about what you will eat or what you will drink. Do not worry about your body and what you will put on. Life is more than food. The body is more than clothing.

"Look at the birds of the air. They do not plant seeds or gather food into barns. Yet your heavenly Father feeds them. You are worth more than they are.

"Can you add a single hour to your life? Do you worry about clothes? Think about the flowers of the field. They do not work or spin to make their clothing. Yet even Solomon in all his glory was not dressed like one of these. If God clothes the grass of the field, which is alive today and tomorrow is gone, He will give you clothes, O you of little faith.

"Do not worry. Do not say, 'What shall we eat?' or 'What shall we drink?' or 'What shall we wear?' Your heavenly Father knows you need all these things. But seek first the kingdom of God and His righteousness. And all these things will be given to you.

"Do not worry about tomorrow. Tomorrow will have its own trouble."

Ask
What does Jesus say about the birds?

What does Jesus say about the flowers?

What does Jesus say about worry?

Do
Sit by a window and watch the birds. What are they eating?

Look for flowers. What are they wearing?

Pray
Heavenly Father, thank You for giving me Jesus, who takes away my worry and my sins. Help me to trust that You will give me all the things I need each day. Amen.

Jesus Feeds Five Thousand People

signs

denarii

barley

John 6

One day after teaching, Jesus went away to the other side of the Sea of Galilee. A large crowd followed Him. For they had seen the miracles and signs He was doing for the sick.

Jesus went up on the mountain. There He sat down with His disciples. Now the Passover, the feast of the Jews, was coming soon. Jesus looked up. He saw a large crowd was coming toward Him.

So Jesus said to Philip, "Where are we to buy bread, so that these people may eat?" He said this to test Philip, for He knew what He would do.

Philip said, "Two hundred denarii would not buy enough bread for each person to get a little."

Ask

What food did the boy share?

What did Jesus do with the food?

How does God care for you?

Do

Go on a "thankful hunt" in your house. As you walk from room to room, name things for which you are thankful.

When you finish, say a prayer together.

Pray

Dear Jesus, thank You for taking care of all my needs each day now and forever. Amen.

Andrew said, "There is a boy here who has five barley loaves and two fish. But what are five barley loaves and two fish for so many people?"

Jesus said, "Have the people sit down."

Now there was grass in the place. So the men sat down, about five thousand of them. Jesus took the loaves. Then He gave thanks. He gave the bread to those who were seated. He also did this with the fish. They had as much as they wanted.

When they were full, Jesus told His disciples, "Gather up the leftovers."

So they gathered them and filled twelve baskets with pieces left over from the five barley loaves. The people saw this miracle as a sign. They said, "Jesus is indeed the Prophet who is to come into the world!"

Jesus Sends the Seventy-two

Luke 10

The Lord picked seventy-two special workers. He sent them to visit places ahead of Him. They went two by two, into every town and place where He was about to go.

Jesus said, "Carry no moneybag. Carry no knapsack. Carry no sandals. Greet no one on the road. Whatever house you enter, first say, 'Peace be to this house!' Stay in the same house. Eat and drink what they provide. For the worker should get his pay. Do not go from house to house.

"When you enter a town and they welcome you, eat what is set before you. Heal the sick. And say to them, 'The kingdom of God has come near to you.'

moneybag

knapsack

kingdom of God

rejects

Ask

Where is Jesus sending these special workers?

What did He want them to do?

Who tells you about Jesus and His kingdom?

Do

Use puppets you have or make stick puppets. Role-play what you could say to people about Jesus.

Pray

Dear Jesus, thank You for pastors and teachers who tell me of Your love. I rejoice that my name is written in heaven. Amen.

"When you enter a town and they do not want you, say, 'Even the dust on our feet we wipe off. But we want you to know that the kingdom of God has come near.'

"The one who hears you hears Me. The one who rejects you rejects Me. The one who rejects Me rejects the Father who sent Me."

Later, the seventy-two returned with joy! They said, "Lord, even demons must do what we say in Your name."

Jesus said, "Do not rejoice in this. Rejoice that your names are written in heaven."

That same hour Jesus rejoiced. He said, "I thank You, My heavenly Father, that You have shown these things to the disciples. Yes, Father, for this was Your gracious will."

Then He turned to His disciples. He said, "Blessed are the eyes that see what you see!"

The Good Samaritan

inherit

soul

mercy

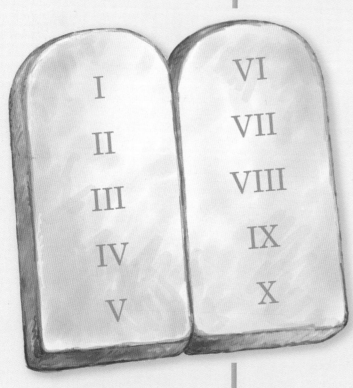

Luke 10

A lawyer asked Jesus, "Teacher, what shall I do to inherit eternal life?"

Jesus said, "What is in the Law?"

The lawyer said, "Love the Lord your God with all your heart and with all your soul and with all your strength and with all your mind. And love your neighbor as yourself."

Jesus said, "You are correct. Do this and you will live."

But the lawyer said to Jesus, "And who is my neighbor?"

Jesus answered with a story.

He said, "A man was going down from Jerusalem to Jericho. Robbers stripped him and beat him. They left him half dead.

"A priest was going down that road. When he saw him, he passed by on the other side. So did another worker from the temple.

Ask

What did the lawyer ask Jesus?

What did the Samaritan do for the man who was robbed?

Who has shown you mercy? What did they do?

Do

Think of something kind you can do for your neighbor.

Whom can you help?

Pray

Dear Jesus, I am not always nice to my neighbors. Forgive me and help me to think of good things I can do for them. Amen.

"But when a Samaritan saw the man, he felt sorry for his suffering. He went to him and wrapped his wounds. He poured oil and wine on them. Then he set the man on his animal. He took him to an inn.

"The next day, he took out some money and gave it to the innkeeper. The Samaritan said, 'Take care of him. If you spend more, I will repay you when I come back.' "

Jesus asked, "Which of these three, do you think, was a neighbor to the man who was robbed?"

The lawyer said, "The one who showed him mercy."

Jesus said, "Go, and show mercy too."

The Good Shepherd

John 10; Psalm 23

Some Pharisees asked Jesus who He was and what He came to do. He said He cares for people the way a shepherd cares for His sheep.

Jesus said, "I am the good shepherd. The good shepherd lays down His life for the sheep. I know My own and My own know Me. I lay down My life for the sheep."

It was winter, and Jesus was walking in the temple. The Jews gathered around Him. And they said, "If You are the Christ, tell us so we can understand."

Jesus answered, "I told you, and you do not believe. The works that I do in My Father's name tell about Me. But you do not believe. My sheep hear My voice, and I know them. They follow Me. I give them eternal life, and they will never perish. No one will snatch them out of My hand."

Many years before, King David wrote a psalm about the Lord. It is called the Shepherd Psalm or Psalm 23.

Pharisees

shepherd

eternal life

perish

soul

righteousness

anoint

A Psalm of David

The Lord is my shepherd;
  I shall not want.

  He makes me lie down in green
  pastures.

He leads me beside still waters.

  He restores my soul.

He leads me in paths of righteousness
  for His name's sake.

Even though I walk through
  the valley of the shadow of death,

I will fear no evil, for You are
  with me.

  Your rod and Your staff,
  they comfort me.

You prepare a table before me
  in the presence of my enemies.

You anoint my head with oil.

  My cup overflows.

Surely goodness and mercy
  shall follow me
  all the days of my life.

And I shall dwell in the house of the
  Lord forever.

Ask
What does Jesus
call Himself?

What does the good
shepherd do?

What did Jesus
do for you?

Do
Sing "I Am Jesus'
Little Lamb."

Pray
Jesus,
my dear Shepherd,
watch over me.
Love me every day
the same. I love
You. Amen.

Jesus and the Little Children

receives

separate

Mark 9–10

Jesus and the disciples came to Capernaum. And when He was in the house, He asked them, "What were you talking about on the way?" But they kept silent. For on the way they had argued about who was the greatest.

Jesus sat down. He called the twelve disciples. He said to them, "If anyone would be first, he must be last of all. He must be servant of all."

Then Jesus took a child. He put him in the midst of them. He took the child in His arms. Jesus said to the disciples, "Whoever receives a child in My name receives Me. Whoever receives Me, receives not Me, but God who sent Me."

Jesus taught the crowds about family.

Jesus said, "God created people male and female. 'Therefore a man shall leave his father and mother. He shall hold onto his wife. The two shall become one flesh.' They are no longer two but one flesh. What God has joined together, let man not separate."

Ask

Whom are the children going to see?

What did Jesus' disciples say?

What does Jesus say to them and to you?

Do

Jesus loves children.

Name the children you know.

After you name each one, say, "Jesus loves (insert a child's name)."

Pray

Dear Jesus, thank You for loving me. Thank You for being my Savior too. Amen.

The crowds were bringing children to Jesus that He might touch them. The disciples rebuked them. But when Jesus saw it, He was angry. He said to the disciples, "Let the children come to Me. Do not hinder them. For to such belongs the kingdom of God. Truly, I say to you, whoever does not receive the kingdom of God like a child shall not enter it."

And He took the children in His arms. He blessed them, laying His hands on them.

The Triumphal Entry

Matthew 21

humble

mounted

cloaks

Hosanna

stirred up

The crowd drew near to Jerusalem. They came to the Mount of Olives. Then Jesus sent two disciples. He said to them, "Go into the village in front of you. You will find a donkey tied, and a colt with her. Untie them and bring them to Me." This took place to fulfill what was spoken by the prophet:

"Behold, your king is coming to you.

He is humble and mounted on a donkey."

The disciples went and did as Jesus said. They brought the donkey and the colt. They put their cloaks on the donkeys, and Jesus sat on them.

Most of the crowd spread their cloaks on the road. Others cut branches from the trees and spread them on the road. And the crowds were shouting, "Hosanna to the Son of David! Blessed is He who comes in the name of the Lord! Hosanna in the highest!"

When Jesus entered Jerusalem, the whole city was stirred up. People said, "Who is this?"

And the crowds said, "This is the prophet Jesus. He is from Nazareth of Galilee."

Jesus entered the temple. He drove out all who sold and bought in the temple. But the blind and the lame came to Jesus. And He healed them.

The chief priests and the scribes saw the wonderful things that Jesus did. They saw the children crying out in the temple, "Hosanna to the Son of David!" The leaders became mad. They said to Jesus, "Do You hear what these children are saying?"

Jesus said to them, "Yes; have you never read in the Psalms,

" 'Out of the mouth of infants and nursing babies God has prepared praise'?"

Ask

What animal did Jesus ride into Jerusalem?

What did the crowd do when Jesus came by?

How did the people praise God?

Do

Wave streamers or scarves and say, "Hosanna" or "Lord, save us."

Pray

Dear Jesus, You are my Savior who has come triumphantly to save me. I will sing to You and praise You too. Amen.

The Lord's Supper

Luke 21–22

Passover

betray

reclined at table

remembrance

covenant

Every day, Jesus was teaching in the temple. But at night He stayed on the mount called Olivet. Then early in the morning all the people came to Jesus in the temple to hear Him.

Now the feast drew near. It is called the Passover.

The chief priests and the scribes were seeking how to put Jesus to death. Judas went to the chief priests and officers. Judas told them he would betray Jesus to them. And they were glad. They agreed to give Judas money.

Then came the day on which the Passover lamb had to be sacrificed. So Jesus sent Peter and John, saying, "Go and prepare the Passover for us. Then we may eat it."

Then the hour of the feast came. Jesus reclined at table. The apostles were with Him. He said to them, "I have desired to eat this Passover with you before I suffer. For I tell you I will not eat it until it is fulfilled in the kingdom of God."

Ask

Look at the story picture. What are Jesus and His disciples doing?

What is Jesus saying?

Who will eat the bread and drink the wine?

Do

Ask a parent to help you make unleavened bread. Unleavened bread is similar to the bread Jesus gave His friends and to the bread we use in Holy Communion.

Pray

Dear Jesus, help me to remember always that You died on the cross for me. Amen.

Jesus took bread. When He had given thanks, He broke it. He gave it to them. And He said, "This is My body, which is given for you. Do this in remembrance of Me."

And likewise He took the cup after they had eaten. He said, "This cup is poured out for you. It is the new covenant in My blood. But behold, the hand of him who betrays Me is with Me on the table."

And the disciples began to question one another. They wondered which of them it could be. ✛

Peter Denies Jesus

Mark 14

After supper, the disciples sang a hymn. Then they went out to the Mount of Olives. Jesus said, "You will all fall away. For it is written, 'I will strike the shepherd, and the sheep will be scattered.' But after I am raised up, I will go before you to Galilee."

Peter said to Him, "They may all fall away. But I will not."

And Jesus said to him, "Truly, I tell you, it will happen this very night. Before the rooster crows twice, you will deny Me three times."

They went to a place called Gethsemane. And Jesus said to His disciples, "Sit here while I pray."

Late at night, Judas came. With him came a crowd with swords and clubs. Now Judas had given a sign. He said, "The one I will kiss is the man. Catch Him."

Judas went up to Jesus at once. He said, "Rabbi!" And he kissed Him. And they laid hands on Jesus and took Him. And all the disciples left Jesus and ran away.

hymn

Rabbi

condemned

Galilean

The crowd led Jesus to the high priest. Peter followed at a distance. He went right into the courtyard of the high priest.

Some people told lies about Jesus. But Jesus remained silent. He made no answer.

The high priest asked Him, "Are you the Christ, the Son of the Blessed?"

Then Jesus said, "I am."

And they all condemned Him to death.

Peter was below in the courtyard. One of the servant girls saw Peter warming himself. She said, "You were with Jesus."

But he denied it. "I don't know what you mean," Peter said. And he went out into the gateway. And the rooster crowed.

Then the servant girl said to others, "This man is one of them."

But again Peter denied it.

Later, others again said to Peter, "You are one of them. For you are a Galilean."

But Peter began to swear, "I do not know this man." And immediately the rooster crowed a second time.

Peter remembered. Jesus had said to him, "Before the rooster crows twice, you will deny Me three times." And Peter wept.

Ask

What did the people ask Peter? Did Peter tell the truth?

Do

Learn to make the sign of the cross. Crosses remind us that Jesus forgives us. Remember, Jesus is ready to forgive us when we do not tell the truth.

Pray

Dear Jesus, sometimes I am afraid too. Sometimes I do not tell the truth. Please forgive me. Thank You for loving me. Amen.

The Passion of Christ

passion

bound

governor

crucified

innocent

Matthew 27

When morning came, all the chief priests and the elders of the people made plans against Jesus. They wanted to put Him to death. So they bound Him. They led Jesus away to Pilate the governor.

Now Jesus stood before the governor. The governor asked Him, "Are You the King of the Jews?"

Jesus said, "You have said so." But He gave him no other answer. So the governor was greatly amazed.

At the feast the governor often released a prisoner whom the crowd wanted. The governor had a prisoner called Barabbas. He had killed people. So when the crowd gathered, Pilate said, "Whom do you want me to release for you: Barabbas, or Jesus?"

They said, "Barabbas."

Pilate said to them, "Then what shall I do with Jesus?"

Ask

What did the people want Pilate to do to Jesus?

For whom did Jesus die on the cross?

Do

Count the crosses in your home.

Each time you find one, say, "Jesus died for me."

Pray

Dear Jesus, I am sad when I see pictures that show how people were mean to You. Thank You, Jesus, for suffering and dying on the cross to take away my sins and give me a home in heaven. Amen.

They all said, "Let Him be crucified!"

And he said, "Why, what evil has He done?"

But they shouted all the more, "Let Him be crucified!"

So Pilate took water and washed his hands before the crowd. He said, "I am innocent of this man's blood. See to it yourselves."

And all the people answered, "His blood be on us and on our children!"

Then Pilate released Barabbas.

The soldiers of the governor took Jesus. They stripped Him. They put a red robe on Him. They twisted a crown of thorns. They put it on His head and put a reed in His right hand. And kneeling before Him, they mocked Him. They said, "Hail, King of the Jews!" And they spit on Him and struck Him on the head.

Then the soldiers led Jesus away to crucify Him. ✠

Jesus Dies and Lives Again

Luke 23–24

criminals

dazzling

apparel

The soldiers led Jesus away. They seized Simon of Cyrene and laid the cross on him. He carried it behind Jesus.

Two criminals were led away to be put to death with Jesus. They came to the place that is called The Skull. There they crucified Jesus and the criminals. One was on His right, and one was on His left.

And Jesus said, "Father, forgive them. For they do not know what they do."

The people stood by, watching. But the rulers and the soldiers mocked Jesus.

One of the criminals said to Jesus, "Are You not the Christ? Save Yourself and us!"

But the other said, "Do you not fear God? This man has done nothing wrong."

Ask

Where are
the women
in the picture?

What are the
angels saying
to the women?

Where is Jesus?

Do

Blow Easter
bubbles.

What's inside the
bubble? Pop one
and find out.

The bubbles are
empty. The tomb
was empty too.

Pray

Dear Jesus,
You can do
anything! You
even can come
back to life!
Thank You
for dying to pay
for my sins.
Thank You
for making it
possible for me
to live forever in
heaven with You.
Amen.

And he said, "Jesus, remember me when You come into Your kingdom."

And Jesus said, "Truly, I say to you, today you will be with Me in Paradise."

There was darkness over the whole land. Then Jesus called out with a loud voice. He said, "Father, into Your hands I commit My spirit!" And He breathed His last.

Now there was a man named Joseph. He took down Jesus' body. He wrapped it. And he laid Jesus in a tomb cut in stone. The women who had come with Jesus from Galilee followed. They saw the tomb.

On the first day of the week, the women went to the tomb. They found the stone rolled away from the tomb. But when they went in they did not find the body of the Lord Jesus.

Then, behold, two men stood by them in dazzling apparel. The men said to the women, "Why do you seek the living among the dead? Jesus is not here. He has risen!" ✠

The Resurrection of Jesus

John 20

linen cloths

Rabboni

My brothers

Early on the first day of the week, Mary Magdalene came to the tomb. It was still dark. She saw that the stone had been taken away from the tomb.

So she ran back to Peter and another disciple. She said, "They have taken the Lord. We do not know where they have laid Him."

So Peter ran with the other disciple to the tomb. The other disciple reached the tomb first. He stooped to look in and saw the linen cloths.

Then Peter went into the tomb. He saw the linen cloths. The face cloth was folded up by itself.

Then the other disciple also went in. He saw and believed. Then the disciples went home.

But Mary stood crying outside the tomb. As she wept she stooped to look into the tomb. There she saw two angels in white. One angel was at the head and one at the feet of where Jesus' body had been laid.

They said, "Woman, why are you weeping?"

She said, "They have taken my Lord. I do not know where they have laid Him." Then she turned and saw Jesus. But she did not recognize Him.

Jesus said, "Woman, why are you weeping? Whom are you seeking?"

Mary thought the man was the gardener. She said, "Sir, if You have carried Jesus away, tell me where He is."

Jesus said, "Mary."

Then she said, "Rabboni!" (which means Teacher).

Jesus said, "Do not hold on to Me. Instead, go to My brothers. Say that I am going to My Father and your Father. I am going to My God and your God."

Mary Magdalene went and told the disciples, "I have seen the Lord." ✝

Ask

Who went to the tomb early on Easter morning?

What was Mary Magdalene's surprise on Easter?

Do

Make play dough Easter eggs and hide them.

Ask your family to hunt for the eggs. When all the eggs are found, tell your family about Mary's Easter surprise.

Pray

Dear Jesus, I am so glad You are alive. Help me tell others this good news. Amen.

Jesus Appears on the Emmaus Road

village

tomb

redeem

vision

vanished

Luke 24

On the day Jesus rose from the dead, two men were going to a village named Emmaus. It was about seven miles from Jerusalem. As they walked, they talked about Jesus' death and the empty tomb.

While they were talking, Jesus came near. He walked on with them. But the two men did not know it was Jesus.

Jesus said, "What are you talking about?"

They stood still. They looked sad. Then Cleopas said, "Don't You know what things have happened these days?"

He said to them, "What things?"

They said, "Things about Jesus. Our priests and rulers put Him on a cross to die.

"He did many wonderful things. We had hoped that He was the one to redeem Israel. It is the third day since He died. And some women amazed us. They were at the tomb early this morning. When they did not find His body, they came back. They said they had seen a vision of angels. The angels said Jesus was alive.

Ask

What happened while the two men were walking to Emmaus?

What did Jesus do for them?

What happened after Jesus vanished?

Do

Choose a partner. Take a walk and retell the Bible story.

Pray

Dear Jesus, thank You for giving me Your Word so I can hear about what You did for me. I am so happy You are alive! Amen.

"Some people with us went to the tomb. They did not see Jesus there."

Jesus said to them, "But Jesus had to suffer." And He explained the Scriptures about Himself.

When they came near the village, Jesus acted as if He were going farther. But the two men said, "Stay with us. For it is evening. The day is almost over."

So Jesus stayed with them. When He was at the table, He took the bread and blessed it. Then He broke it and gave it to them. At once, they were able to recognize Him. But He vanished from their sight.

They said to one another, "He helped us understand the Scriptures." Then, they got up and returned to Jerusalem. They found the eleven disciples, who said, "The Lord has risen indeed! He has appeared to Simon!" Then the men told what had happened on the road. They told the disciples how they saw it was Jesus when He broke the bread. ✝

Jesus Appears to Thomas

John 20

On Easter evening, the disciples locked the doors. They were afraid of the Jews.

Jesus came and stood among them. He said, "Peace be with you." Then He showed them His hands and His side.

The disciples were glad. Jesus said to them again, "Peace be with you. As the Father has sent Me, I am sending you."

Then He breathed on them and said, "I give you the Holy Spirit. If you forgive the sins of anyone, they are forgiven. If you do not forgive their sins, they are not forgiven."

Thomas was not with them when Jesus came. So the other disciples told him, "We have seen the Lord."

But Thomas said, "Unless I see in His hands the nail marks, and place my finger in them, and place my hand into His side, I will never believe."

Eight days later, Jesus' disciples were inside again. This time Thomas was with them. The doors were locked, but Jesus stood there. He said, "Peace be with you."

appears

Holy Spirit

signs

275

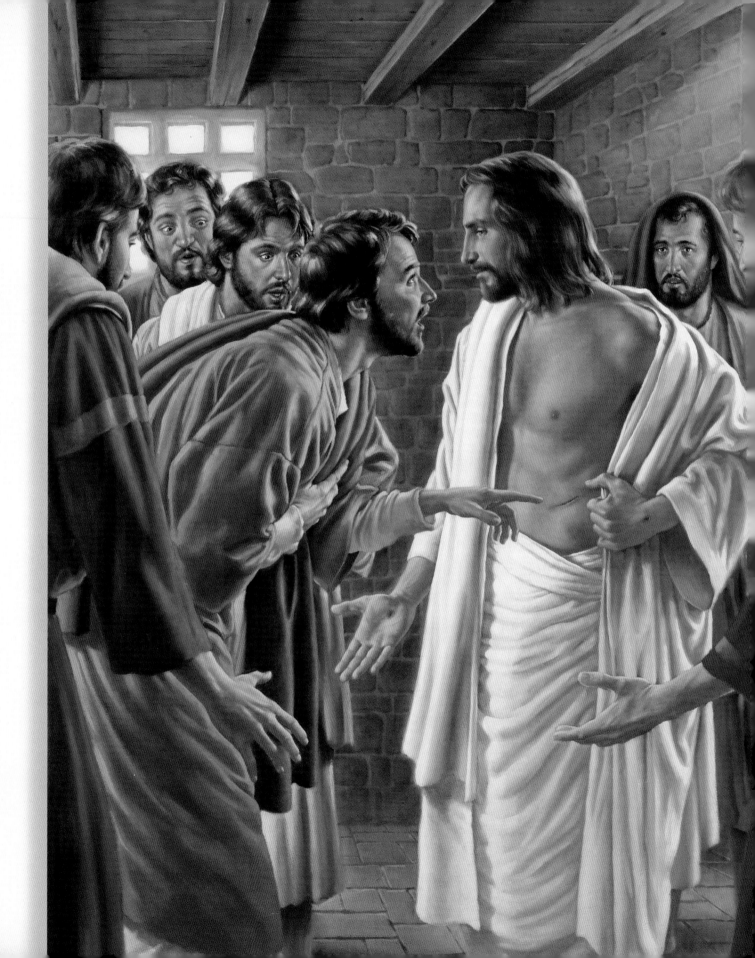

Then He said to Thomas, "Put your finger here, and see My hands. Put your hand in My side. Believe."

Thomas said, "My Lord and my God!"

Jesus said, "Do you believe because you see Me? Blessed are those who have not seen Me and yet believe."

Jesus did many other signs with His disciples. Not all of them are written in this book. But these are written so that you may believe that Jesus is the Son of God. And by believing you may have life in His name. ✝

Ask

What does Thomas say to his friends before he sees Jesus?

What does Thomas say to Jesus after he sees Jesus?

Do

Look carefully at the picture of Thomas and Jesus.

Can you find the nail prints on Jesus' hands?

Can you find the scar on Jesus' side?

Pray

Dear Jesus, thank You for loving Thomas so much and helping him to believe that You were alive. Help me believe in You forever and ever. Amen.

Jesus Appears in Galilee

shore

cast

John 21

One day after Easter, Peter and some of the other disciples were together. Peter said, "I am going fishing."

They said, "We will go with you." They got into the boat. But that night they did not catch any fish.

As daylight was coming, Jesus stood on the shore. The disciples did not know that it was Jesus.

Jesus said, "Do you have any fish?"

They answered Him, "No."

He said, "Cast the net on the right side of the boat. You will find some."

So they threw the net in the water on the right side of the boat.

Ask

What were the men in the boat doing?

Who was on the land?

How did Jesus show His love in the story?

Do

Play Go Fish.

Talk about how Jesus used fish to show how much He cared for His friends.

How does Jesus show His love for us?

Pray

Dear Jesus, I am so happy that You are alive, really alive! Amen.

Now they had so many fish that they were not able to haul in the net. One of the disciples said to Peter, "It is the Lord!"

When Peter heard that it was the Lord, he threw himself into the water. The other disciples came in the boat, dragging the net full of fish.

They got out on land and saw a fire with fish on it. There was bread too. Jesus said to them, "Bring some of the fish that you have just caught."

Peter went on the boat. He hauled the net to shore. It was full of large fish, 153 of them. There were so many fish, but the net was not torn.

Jesus said to them, "Come and have breakfast."

Jesus took the bread and gave it to the disciples. Then He gave them the fish.

This was the third time Jesus showed Himself to the disciples after He was raised from the dead. ✝

Jesus Ascends into Heaven

John 21; Acts 1

When Jesus was arrested, all the disciples ran away. Peter denied Jesus three times. But now things would be different.

Jesus said to Peter, "Do you love Me?"

He said, "Yes, Lord. You know that I love You."

Jesus said, "Feed My lambs."

A second time Jesus said, "Peter, do you love Me?"

Peter said, "Yes, Lord. You know that I love You."

Jesus said, "Tend My sheep." A third time Jesus said, "Peter, do you love Me?"

Peter was very sad that Jesus had asked him the third time. Peter said, "Lord, You know everything. You know that I love You."

Jesus said, "Feed My sheep." Later, Jesus said to Peter, "Follow Me."

Peter turned. He saw another disciple whom Jesus loved. He was following them. Peter said, "Lord, what about this man?"

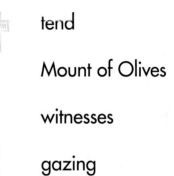

tend

Mount of Olives

witnesses

gazing

Jesus said to Peter, "What is that to you? You follow Me!"

Jesus showed the disciples that He was alive for forty days. He spoke to them about the kingdom of God.

Jesus also told the disciples to stay in Jerusalem. They were to wait there for the promise of the Father. Jesus said, "You will be baptized with the Holy Spirit in a few days."

Later, Jesus led them to the Mount of Olives. They asked, "Now will You bring back the kingdom to Israel?"

He said, "You do not need to know what God does. But you will get power when the Holy Spirit comes to you. You will speak God's Word in Jerusalem. You will be My witnesses to the end of the earth."

As the disciples were looking, Jesus was lifted up. Then a cloud took Him out of sight.

The disciples were gazing into heaven as Jesus went up. And behold! Two men stood by them in white robes.

The men said, "Men of Galilee, why are you looking into heaven? Jesus will come back the same way as you saw Him go into heaven." ✝

Ask

What question did Jesus ask Peter three times?

How did Jesus show His love?

Where did Jesus go?

Will Jesus come back?

Do

Cut a cloud out of paper.

Write these words on the cloud: [Jesus said,] "I am with you always" (Matthew 28:20).

Play hide-and-seek with the cloud. Remember that even though Jesus has gone to heaven, He promises to be with us always.

Pray

Dear Jesus, thank You for going to prepare a wonderful home for me in heaven. Help me to listen to Your Word while I wait for You to come again. Amen.

God Sends the Holy Spirit

Acts 2

Pentecost

tongues

languages

mocked

prophesy

The day of Pentecost came. The disciples were all together in one place. And suddenly there came from heaven a sound like a mighty rushing wind. It filled the entire house where they were sitting. And tongues as of fire appeared to them. The fire rested on each one of them. And they were all filled with the Holy Spirit. The Spirit helped them to speak in other languages.

Now there were Jews dwelling in Jerusalem. They were men from every nation under heaven. And at this sound the Jews came together. They were amazed, because each one was hearing them speak in his own language.

And they said, "Are not all these who are speaking Galileans? And how is it that we hear them telling in our own languages the mighty works of God?"

And all were amazed. They said to one another, "What does this mean?"

Ask

Who are the people in the story picture?

What is over their heads?

What does Peter tell the people?

Whom did God send to help Peter tell about Jesus?

Do

God wants people who speak other languages to hear about Jesus.

Can you say something in another language?

Pray

Dear Jesus, thank You for sending the Holy Spirit. Forgive my sins and help me share Your love with others. Amen.

But others mocked. They said, "They are filled with new wine."

But Peter stood with the eleven. He lifted up his voice and addressed them. "Men of Judea and all who dwell in Jerusalem, listen to my words. This is what was said through the prophet Joel:

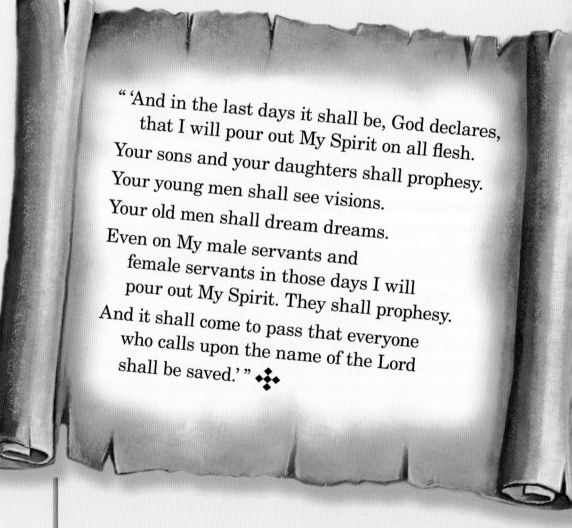

" 'And in the last days it shall be, God declares, that I will pour out My Spirit on all flesh. Your sons and your daughters shall prophesy. Your young men shall see visions. Your old men shall dream dreams. Even on My male servants and female servants in those days I will pour out My Spirit. They shall prophesy. And it shall come to pass that everyone who calls upon the name of the Lord shall be saved.' "

Philip and the Ethiopian

Acts 8

Now an angel of the Lord said to Philip, "Rise and go toward the south. Take the road that goes down from Jerusalem to Gaza." (This is a desert place.)

And Philip rose and went. And there was an Ethiopian, a court official of Candace, the queen. He was in charge of all her treasure. He had come to Jerusalem to worship. Now he was returning, seated in his chariot. He was reading the prophet Isaiah.

And the Spirit said to Philip, "Go over and join this chariot."

So Philip ran to him. He heard him reading from Isaiah the prophet. He asked, "Do you understand what you are reading?"

And he said, "How can I, unless someone guides me?" And he invited Philip to come up and sit with him.

Ethiopian

chariot

Scripture

shearer

Now the passage of the Scripture that he was reading was this:

"Like a sheep He was led to death and like a lamb before its shearer is silent, so He does not open His mouth."

And the Ethiopian said to Philip, "About whom, I ask you, does the prophet say this? About himself? About someone else?"

Then Philip opened his mouth. Beginning with this Scripture he told the Ethiopian the good news about Jesus.

And as they were going along the road they came to some water. The Ethiopian said, "See, here is water! What prevents me from being baptized?" And he commanded the chariot to stop.

Philip and the Ethiopian both went down into the water. Philip baptized him. And when they came up out of the water, the Spirit of the Lord carried Philip away.

The Ethiopian saw Philip no more and went on his way rejoicing. But Philip found himself at Azotus. He preached the Gospel to all the towns by the sea.

Ask

Look at the picture. What is the man reading?

Whom does God send to help the man learn about Jesus?

When they came to the water, what did the man ask Philip to do?

Do

Philip ran to catch the Ethiopian's chariot.

Run around and thank God for His Word.

Pray

Dear God, thank You for working through Your Word and Baptism to make the man from Ethiopia Your child. Thank You for sending the Holy Spirit to give me faith in Jesus through Your Word and Baptism. Amen.

The Conversion of Saul

conversion

persecuting

Gentiles

Acts 9

Saul heard Stephen preach. It made him mad. Saul went to the high priest. He asked him for help to act against anyone found belonging to the Way of Jesus. Saul would bring them bound to Jerusalem.

Now as Saul went on his way, he came to Damascus. Suddenly a light from heaven flashed around him. He fell to the ground. A voice said to him, "Saul, Saul, why are you persecuting Me?"

He said, "Who are You, Lord?"

And he heard, "I am Jesus, whom you are persecuting. Rise and enter the city. You will be told what you are to do."

The men who were traveling with Saul stood speechless. They heard the voice but saw no one. Saul rose from the ground. His eyes were opened, but he saw nothing. So the men led him by the hand into Damascus. For three days Saul could not see. He also did not eat or drink.

Now there was a disciple at Damascus named Ananias. The Lord said to him in a vision, "Ananias."

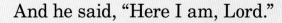

Ask

Who talked to Saul on the road?

What did Jesus tell Saul?

Where does Jesus speak to us?

Do

Close your eyes. Ask someone to guide you around as you both sing a song about Jesus.

Pray

Dear Jesus,
I am glad You loved Saul so much that You changed him from an enemy to Your friend. Thank You for loving me that much, too, and for calling me to be Your child through Baptism and Your Word. Amen.

And he said, "Here I am, Lord."

The Lord said to him, "Rise and look for a man named Saul. Behold, he is praying. He has seen a vision. A man named Ananias will come. He will lay his hands on him so that he might have his sight."

But Ananias answered, "Lord, I have heard he has done much evil to Your saints at Jerusalem."

But the Lord said, "Go, for he will carry My name before the Gentiles and kings and the children of Israel. For I will show him how much he must suffer for the sake of My name."

So Ananias departed. He entered the house, and he laid his hands on Saul. He said, "Brother Saul, the Lord Jesus has sent me. You will be able to see again and be filled with the Holy Spirit."

Right away Saul could see again. Then he rose and was baptized. He proclaimed Jesus in the prayer houses. He said, "He is the Son of God." And all who heard him were amazed.

So the church had peace and was being built up. ❖❖

Peter's Escape from Prison

Acts 12

Herod the king laid violent hands on some who belonged to the church. He killed James the brother of John with the sword. He saw that it pleased the Jews. So he arrested Peter also. He put him in prison with four squads of soldiers to guard him. But the church prayed to God for Peter.

Herod was about to bring Peter out to judge him. On that very night, Peter was sleeping between two soldiers, bound with two chains. Sentries before the door were guarding the prison. And behold, an angel of the Lord stood next to Peter. A light shone in the cell.

The angel struck Peter on the side and woke him. He said, "Get up quickly." The chains fell off Peter's hands. And the angel said to him, "Dress yourself. Put on your sandals. Wrap your cloak around you and follow me."

And Peter went out and followed the angel. He did not know that what was being done by the angel was real. Peter thought he was seeing a vision.

violent

squads

sentries

insisting

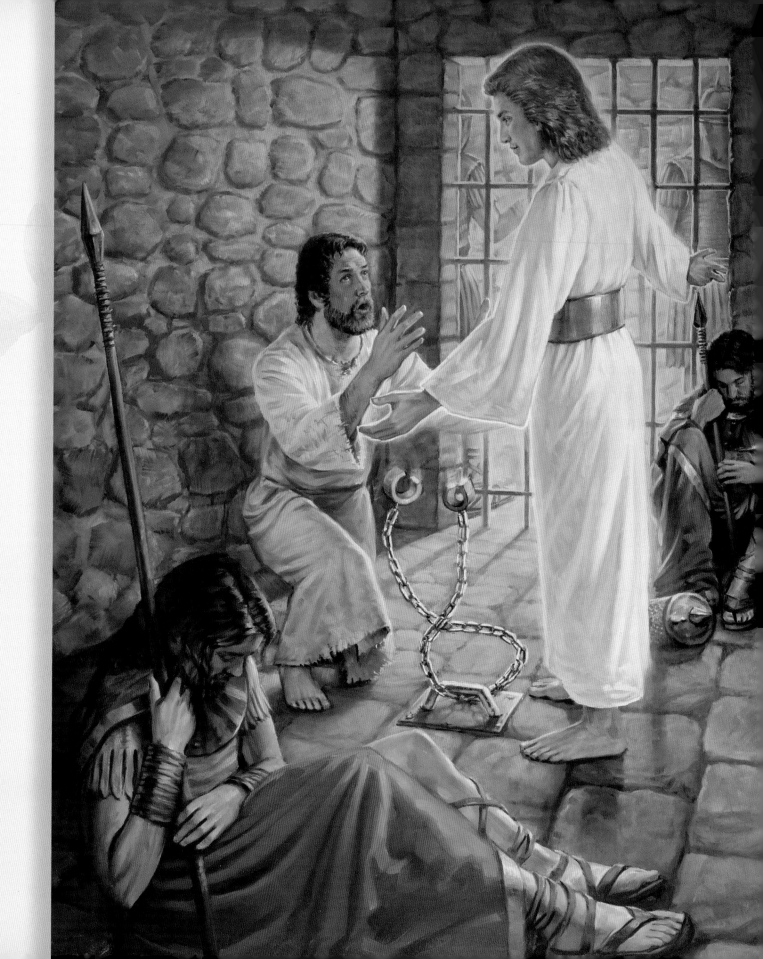

They passed the first and the second guard. They came to the iron gate leading into the city. It opened for them on its own. They went out, and soon the angel left Peter.

When Peter came to himself, he said, "Now I am sure that the Lord has sent His angel. He rescued me from the hand of Herod."

Peter went to the house of Mary. Many were there praying. He knocked at the door of the gateway.

A servant girl named Rhoda came to answer. She knew Peter's voice. In her joy she did not open the gate. She ran in and reported that Peter was standing at the gate.

They said to her, "You are out of your mind." But she kept insisting that it was so.

Peter kept knocking. When they opened the door, they saw him. They were amazed! So the word of God increased and multiplied. ❖❖❖

Ask

Where was Peter?
How did Peter get out of jail?
Who rescues us from our sins?

Do

Draw an angel as a reminder that God sends His angels to watch over us.

Pray

Dear God, thank You for watching over Peter. Thank You for sending angels to watch over me too. Amen.

Paul and Timothy

Acts 15–16; 1 Timothy 1; 2 Timothy 4

mission

accompany

decisions

conscience

Paul chose Silas for a mission trip. The church leaders sent Paul and Silas with the grace of the Lord. So they went through Syria and Cilicia. Paul strengthened the churches. He came to Derbe and to Lystra.

A disciple was there named Timothy. He was the son of a Jewish woman who was a believer. But his father was a Greek. He was well spoken of by the brothers. So Paul wanted Timothy to accompany them.

Paul, Silas, and Timothy went on their way through the cities. They delivered the decisions of the apostles and elders. And the churches were strengthened in the faith. They increased in numbers daily.

Young Timothy became a minister of the Word. He was Paul's trusted friend and worker. Two of Paul's last letters were to Timothy. They show Paul's trust in him and his trust in the Lord.

Paul, an apostle of Christ Jesus by command of God our Savior and of Christ Jesus our hope.

Ask

Who taught Timothy about God?

What did Paul want Timothy to do?

Will God help Timothy?

Do

Shake rhythm instruments and boldly say, "Jesus has saved me."

Pray

Dear Jesus,
You did everything for me. Thank You for taking my punishment and giving me a home in heaven.
Amen.

To Timothy, my true child in the faith:

Grace, mercy, and peace from God the Father and Christ Jesus our Lord.

The aim of our work is love that comes from a pure heart and a good conscience and a sincere faith.

The Lord stood by me and strengthened me, so that through me the message might be fully proclaimed. Then all the Gentiles might hear it.

I was rescued from the lion's mouth. The Lord will rescue me from every evil deed. He will bring me safely into His heavenly kingdom. To Him be the glory forever and ever. Amen.

Lydia

Acts 16; Philippians 1

The Holy Spirit forbade Paul, Timothy, and Silas from preaching the word in Asia Minor. But a vision appeared to Paul at night: a man of Macedonia was standing there. He said, "Come here. Help us!"

When Paul had seen the vision, right away he tried to go there. He decided that God had called them to preach the Gospel in Macedonia.

So Paul and his friends set sail. They came to Philippi. This was a leading city and a Roman colony. They remained in this city some days.

On the Sabbath day Paul and his friends went outside the gate to the riverside. They supposed there was a place of prayer there. They sat down and spoke to the women who had come together.

forbade

colony

One woman who heard Paul was named Lydia. She was from the city of Thyatira. She sold purple goods. She was a worshiper of God. The Lord opened her heart to pay attention to what was said by Paul.

Afterward Lydia was baptized, and her household as well. Then she said to Paul and the others, "If you have judged me to be faithful to the Lord, come to my house and stay."

The church at Philippi became strong. Paul later wrote about them:

I thank my God in all my remembrance of you. I thank Him always in every prayer of mine. I make my prayer for you with joy.

Ask

What are Lydia and her friends doing?

What does Paul tell Lydia?

What happened after Lydia heard about Jesus?

Do

Lydia sold purple cloth. She loved Jesus.

Use a purple crayon to draw a big cross or to write the name of *Jesus*.

Pray

Dear God, thank You for sending people to tell me about Jesus and for making me Your child. Amen.

Paul and Silas in Prison

jailer

fastened

stocks

bonds

uncondemned

Acts 16

At Philippi angry men seized Paul and Silas. They dragged them into the marketplace before the rulers. They said, "These men are Jews. They teach things that are not lawful for us as Romans to accept or practice."

The crowd joined in attacking them. The leaders tore the clothes off them. They gave orders to beat them with rods. And they ordered the jailer to keep them. He put them into the inner prison. He fastened their feet in the stocks.

About midnight Paul and Silas were praying and singing hymns to God. The prisoners were listening to them.

Suddenly there was a great earthquake. The foundations of the prison were shaken! All the doors were opened. Everyone's bonds were unfastened.

The jailer woke. He saw that the prison doors were open. He drew his sword. He was about to kill himself. He thought the prisoners had escaped.

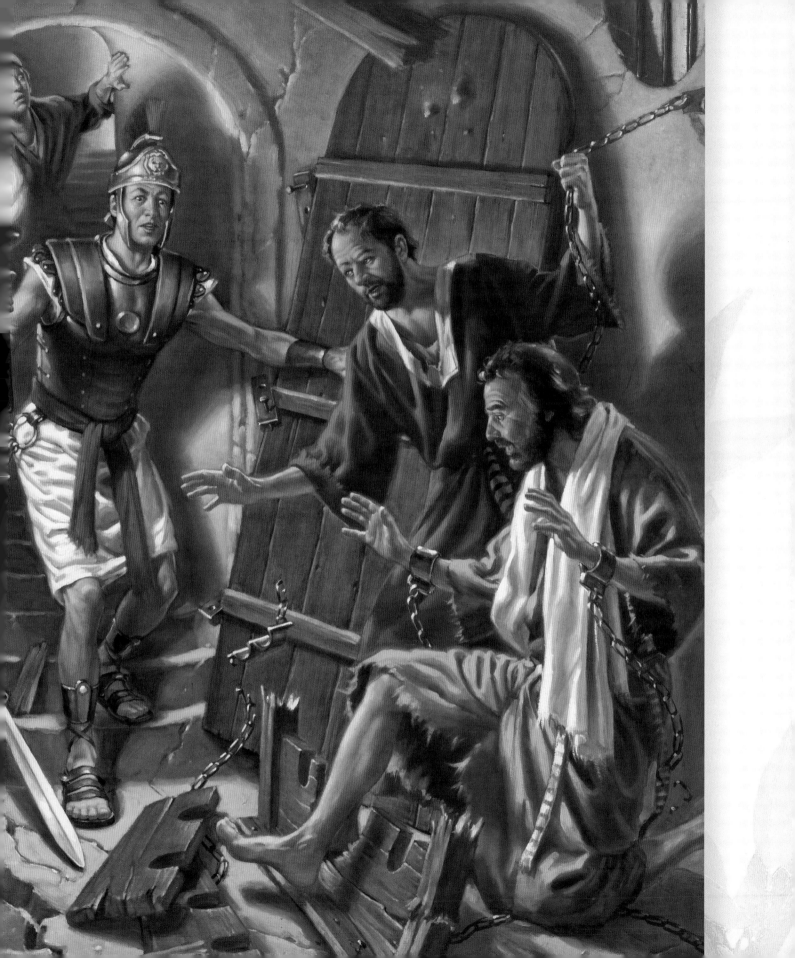

Ask

Where were Paul and Silas?

What happened to their chains?

About whom do Paul and Silas tell the jailer?

What happened at the jailer's house?

Do

Make a brightly colored paper chain.

Decorate the links with crosses.

Drape the chain in a special place as a reminder to pray for those who do not know about Jesus.

Pray

Dear Jesus, help me to listen to Your words from the Bible so I can learn more about You and Your love. When others are in trouble, help me to tell them about You. Amen.

But Paul cried with a loud voice, "Do not harm yourself. We are all here."

The jailer called for lights and rushed in. Trembling with fear he fell down before Paul and Silas. Then he brought them out. He said, "Sirs, what must I do to be saved?"

And they said, "Believe in the Lord Jesus. You will be saved, you and your household." And they spoke the word of the Lord to him and to all who were in his house.

And he took them the same hour of the night and washed their wounds. The jailer was baptized at once, he and all his family. Then he rejoiced along with his entire household that he had believed in God.

But when it was day, the leaders sent the police, saying, "Let those men go."

The jailer reported these words to Paul. He said, "The leaders will let you go. Therefore come out now. Go in peace."

But Paul said to them, "They have beaten us without judging us to be guilty. And we are Roman citizens. No! Let them come themselves and take us out."

So the leaders came and told Paul and Silas they were sorry. Then Paul and Silas went out of the prison.

Paul and Timothy, Lois and Eunice

2 Timothy 1

Paul made it all the way to Rome. He told people there about Jesus. His last letter was for his friend Timothy. It talks about Timothy's family and also a friend.

Paul, an apostle of Christ Jesus by the will of God, according to the promise of life in Christ Jesus.

To Timothy, my beloved child:

Grace, mercy, and peace from God the Father and Christ Jesus our Lord.

I thank God whom I serve. I remember you in my prayers night and day. As I remember your tears, I long to see you. Then I may be filled with joy.

I am reminded of your faith. That faith dwelt first in your grandmother Lois and your mother Eunice. And now, I am sure, it dwells in you as well.

Fan into flame the gift of God. This gift is in you through the laying on of my hands. For God did not give us a spirit of fear but of power and love and self-control.

reminded

self-control

ashamed

abolished

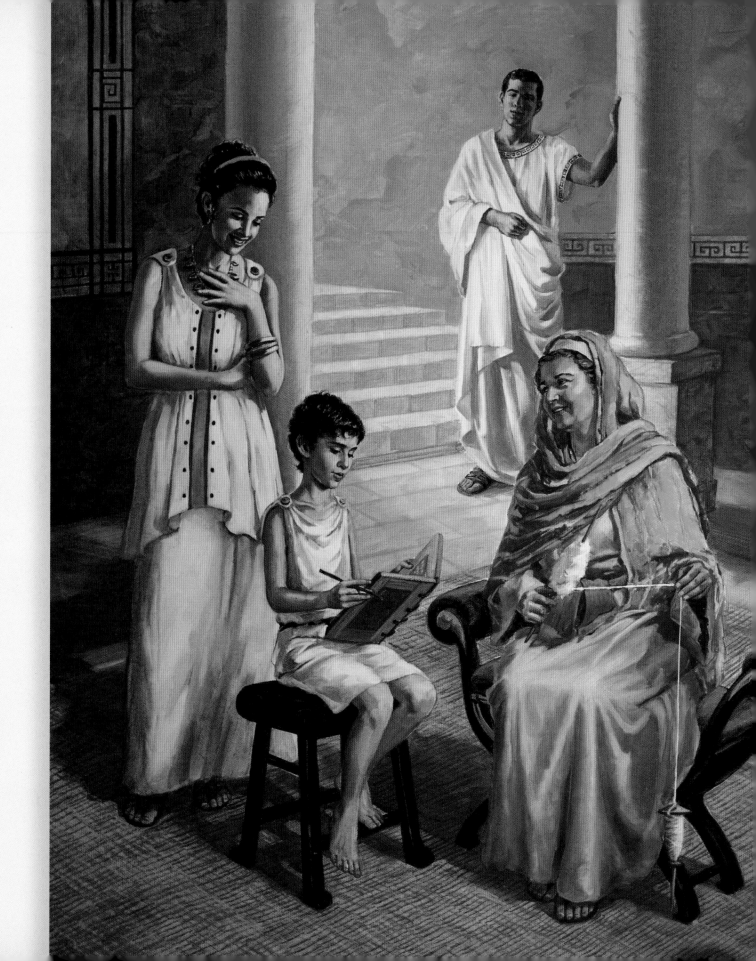

Do not be ashamed of our Lord, nor of me His prisoner. But share in suffering for the Gospel by the power of God. He saved us and called us to a holy calling. He did this not because of our works but because of His own purpose and grace. He gave us grace in Christ Jesus before the ages began. Now grace has been seen in our Savior Christ Jesus. He abolished death and brought life to light through the Gospel.

I was made a teacher for the Gospel. This is why I suffer as I do. But I am not ashamed. I know whom I have believed.

Follow the pattern of the sound words that you have heard from me. Do so in the faith and love that are in Christ Jesus. By the Holy Spirit who dwells within us, guard the teaching entrusted to you. ✠

Ask

What did Paul send Timothy?

Who were Lois and Eunice?

What news did Paul write to Timothy?

Do

Say a prayer to thank God for the people who have taught you about Jesus.

Ask God to give them His power and love.

Pray

Dear Jesus, when I am afraid, remind me of Your power and love. Thank You for faithful pastors and teachers who tell me about Jesus, my Savior. Amen.

John's Vision of Heaven

Revelation 21–22

John wrote about what Jesus showed him.

I saw a new heaven and a new earth.
The first heaven and the first earth
had passed away. And I saw the holy city,
new Jerusalem.

And I heard a loud voice from the throne
of heaven. It said, "Behold, the dwelling
place of God is with man. He will dwell
with them. They will be His people. God
Himself will be with them as their God. He
will wipe away every tear from their eyes.
Death shall be no more. There shall not
be crying or pain anymore."

The Lord said, "Behold, I am making all
things new. Write this down. These words
are trustworthy and true."

Then the angel showed me the river
of the water of life. He showed me the tree
of life with its twelve kinds of fruit.

"And behold," Jesus said. "I am coming
soon. Blessed is the one who keeps the words
of this book."

dwelling place

trustworthy

grace

Ask

Who was talking to John?

What did the angel say?

Whom will we see in heaven?

Do

Look at the picture of John's vision. Tell what you like best about the picture.

Pray

Dear Jesus,
You gave John a beautiful picture of heaven. Thank You for making heaven a special place for me and all Your children. Amen.

I, John, am the one who heard and saw these things. I fell down to worship at the feet of the angel.

But he said to me, "You must not do that! I am a servant with you. Worship God."

Jesus says, "I am the first and the last. Surely I am coming soon."

Amen. Come, Lord Jesus! The grace of the Lord Jesus be with all. Amen.

These stories are written

so that you may believe that

Jesus is the Christ,

the Son of God,

and that by believing you may

have life in His name.

(John 20:31)

Artwork credits